D0765323

SECRETS OF Entrepreneurial Leadership

Building Top Performance Through Trust & Teamwork

Ted Nicholas

FOREWORD BY JOSEPH SUGARMAN
Famed Entrepreneur & Owner of JS&A Group, Inc.

While a great deal of care has been taken to provide accurate and current information, the ideas, suggestions, general principles and conclusions presented in this text are subject to local, state and federal laws and regulations, court cases and any revisions of same. The reader is thus urged to consult legal counsel regarding any points of law—this publication should not be used as a substitute for competent legal advice.

Published by Enterprise • Dearborn,
a division of Dearborn Publishing Group, Inc.

Printed in the United States of America

93 94 95 10 9 8 7 6 5 4 3 2 1

Library of Congress Cataloging-in-Publication Data

Nichols, Ted, 1934–
[Management for entrepreneurs]
Secrets of entrepreneurial leadership / by Ted Nicholas.
p. cm.
Previously published as: Management for entrepreneurs.
Includes index.
ISBN 0-79310-493-9
1. Personnel management. 2. Employee motivation. 3. Trust (Psychology). I. Title. II. Series: Nicholas, Ted, 1934– Management for entrepreneurs.
HF5549.N4715 1992 92-18597
658.4'21—dc20 CIP

Books by Ted Nicholas

The Complete Book of Corporate Forms

The Complete Guide to Business Agreements

The Complete Guide to Consulting Success
(coauthor, Howard Shenson)

The Executive's Business Letter Book

43 Proven Ways To Raise Capital for Your Small Business

The Golden Mailbox: How To Get Rich Direct Marketing Your Product

How To Form Your Own Corporation Without a Lawyer for
Under $75.00

How To Get a Top Job in Tough Times (coauthor, Bethany Waller)

How To Get Your Own Trademark

Secrets of Entrepreneurial Leadership: Building Top Performance
Through Trust and Teamwork

Dedication

Dedicated to my employees, past and present, who have been receptive to new ideas and, as a result, have contributed to my growth as a manager. It is my hope that they have also learned and prospered from our mutual experience.

Table of Contents

Foreword

The entrepreneur is truly the real hero in today's society. From innovation to job creation, entrepreneurs have done more to shape the success of our country than any other single group. And in my judgment, the key reason is leadership.

An entrepreneur is more a true leader and less a manager. Management can be defined as the ability to *utilize people* to accomplish your goals, whereas leadership involves *influencing people* to achieve your goals. Both require different skills, and both are essential to the success of a business.

Entrepreneurial management could easily be an oxymoron. Entrepreneurs by nature are visionaries who often operate by the seat of their pants with very little structure. It's the nature of the beast. And to the pure entrepreneur, management, though not as exciting, by necessity must be incorporated into a business structure.

The innovative attitude of the entrepreneur may also breed distrust and fear or may lead to the development of a staff who showers the boss with adulation or quickly learns his or her odd ways and responds in unconventional behavior—some good, some bad.

The entrepreneur loves the power and risk-taking but does not want those people he or she manages to take the same risks and exercise the same power. On the other hand, the word *management* has a very structured connotation. To the entrepreneur, managing a staff is a real necessity but one that can cramp his or her style. That's what makes this book such an important one for anyone in business—not just entrepreneurs.

Ted Nicholas takes the reader along on several visits to a restaurant where he meets with another entrepreneur to discuss his leadership philosophies. During each meeting topics are raised that every business owner encounters during the course of running a business and managing people. Nicholas shows how style and sensitivity combine to create a trusting atmosphere, encouraged from the top down, and how valuable that can be to a productive and profitable company.

Many of the concepts I found to be very informative and helped me focus on issues that I was unaware were even leadership issues. Other concepts were not new to me but were presented with that special insight that often only a business owner could appreciate.

Ted Nicholas is the consummate entrepreneur. He has started over 20 businesses—from an ice cream enterprise to one of the most successful publishing businesses. Through publishing he has educated thousands of business entrepreneurs, many of whom owe their success to his teachings.

It's not surprising that many of my meetings with Ted were in five-star restaurants enjoying lunch or dinner and discussing our adventures in running our respective businesses. He has always struck me as an incredible mix of entrepreneur and manager—sharing the lessons learned from running so many businesses and from managing so many people. (By the way, he has an incredible appetite.)

Ted Nicholas shares his wealth of experience, his sensitivity to people and the lessons he has learned in a very easy-to-read adventure filled with real-life examples.

If you're like most entrepreneurs and are confused by the challenge of leading people, then you'll appreciate, enjoy and refer often to the chapters presented in this wonderful book. I give it five stars!

—Joseph Sugarman, Chairman
JS&A Group, Inc.

Introduction

Most workers do not trust their bosses.

According to a study done at Boston University, fully 78 percent of American workers are suspicious of management. They feel that it's "us against them." Psychologists involved in the study said these workers spurn innovation and create unrest. Their first loyalty is to themselves, not the firm.

I believe in people and what they can achieve. This book is about helping free some of the greatness that lies within all humans.

The most important component of management is simple. If you trust someone, he or she will tend to be trustworthy. Trust your people. And then they will trust you.

But the opposite is also true. Mistrust breeds more mistrust. Mistrust can become a self-fulfilling prophecy.

Some degree of trust exists in every business at some level. The extent to which a business becomes great depends largely on how high a level of trust can be built among its people. This basic truth applies to the corner grocery store with three employees all the way up to the largest corporation in the world, General Motors.

Great businesses, large or small, have three things in common: (1) the score is clear; (2) the mission is clear; (3) people trust each other.

With these thoughts in mind, I decided to put together this little book.

One day a good friend and tennis partner was having lunch with me when he leaned back in his chair, looked at me quizzically and said: "Ted, I know you run a very successful enterprise. More than that, when I drop by your office I sense something different. It's a busy office, but it's a *happy* office. Your employees seem to like their jobs. Everything's . . . well, vital, alive! I sense it as soon as I put my foot in the door. What's up?"

I smiled and said, "It wasn't always that way. Oh, I was lucky. The first company I started—when I was only 21—made money. I subsequently started 22 others. All but two that followed showed a sizable profit. I made mistakes and tried to learn from them. But when I began my present company, in 1973, I knew *something* was missing, and I suspected it had to do with personal relationships. Maybe I was too authoritarian, issued too many orders, didn't trust my employees . . . and I sensed they didn't really trust me."

"So what did you do?"

"I engaged a group of associates to help me develop an entirely different management style. We worked on the principle that the employees' first loyalty must be to themselves. *Their* success and growth are responsible for the firm's success. With the help of Dr. Luanne Ruona of Self Esteem Associates (Washington, D.C.), we set up a series of meetings in my company and talked about effective communication, problem solving, assertiveness and conflict resolution."

"Were all your employees in on these meetings?"

"At first just the top managers, then a couple of supervisors, but soon everyone."

"It worked?"

"Right away. And it was fascinating to watch groups evolve. As people began to work on various issues, relationships improved. So did productivity and trust."

"I notice you use the word *trust* a lot, Ted."

"I feel it's the key word. So do my employees."

"But does it get results?"

"Yes. In fact, our early meetings—and the ones we have weekly—focus on *results* or *output*. My associates want to know what is expected of them. They like being regarded for results and recognized for their productivity.

"I know your company publishes books and offers services to small businesses. Isn't it harder to measure output in your organization than, say, a manufacturing concern making a tangible product like microwave ovens?"

"Perhaps, but we do it."

"And isn't it easier to do this in a medium-sized company such as yours? Would it work in a small enterprise or a large corporation?"

"I'm convinced, Bill, that it will work in *any size* organization. *Any company can be designed and managed for success.* Everyone's potential can be unleashed and raised to a high level. And a company whose leaders do this can't be stopped!"

"Wow! You really believe this. You know, I'm deeply interested in this subject. I've known for a long time I needed to make a lot of improvements in my printing plant, and I think I can learn a lot from you. Could we talk more about it?"

"I suppose we could over a lunch. But in a brief meeting we'd just cover the basics. We'd have to meet several times to get into real depth."

"Well, Ted, I wouldn't ask you to give all your time and knowledge to me for free. I'd like to pay you a consultant's fee."

"That would be one approach. But let me give it some thought. I'm sure we can work out something we're both comfortable with. Let's plan on lunch next Wednesday, and we can both think about it in the meantime. The two of us could benefit from an idea that's beginning to form in my mind."

"Can't you tell me a little bit about it now, Ted?"

"Well, here is my concept. Why couldn't we meet for lunch once a week and tape our conversations? You could keep notes and transcribe the tapes. Then I'll edit them. We could cover a specific topic each week. And probably we could both grow from it, too. That way, maybe we'll end up with a book I've always wanted to do on management. But before we part, let me jot down for you my list of 20 trust builders."

"It's a date, Ted! Same time, same place?"

"Right! See you next Wednesday."

Nicholas's Twenty Trust Builders

1. Trust your associates and they will tend to be trustworthy.
2. Respect your associates.
3. Inspire your associates with purpose.
4. Let your associates know what is expected of them.
5. Provide your associates with power.
6. Develop a sense of mission.
7. Inspire confidence.
8. Create a productive atmosphere and attitude.
9. Make a contract for commitment.
10. Keep score and measure performance.
11. Share power with your associates.
12. Generate quality communication.
13. Create an atmosphere that encourages free airing and resolution of conflict.
14. Make sure that everyone participates in decision-making processes.
15. Provide an environment that nurtures creativity.
16. Promote good time management.
17. Be sure to define problems before you make resolutions.
18. See that your associates have what's needed to do the job.
19. Help your associates meet their highest-level need for self-fulfillment.
20. Create a strong company culture.

1

Trust—The Glue That Binds

As soon as we had ordered lunch the following Wednesday, Bill and I began discussing the idea of a book. Bill had his tape recorder with him, and I had an outline of topics to be covered.

"I like your outline," Bill said as he studied it.

"Well, we can be flexible and can add or delete topics as we progress."

"Good idea!"

"Incidentally, Bill, I always carry a small note pad with me so I can write down an idea whenever and wherever I am."

"I'll plan to do the same, Ted."

"Good! Now are you ready to roll?"

"Ready!"

"Okay. Let's start with trust in the work environment."

"Ted, I've been thinking about your list this past week. You're sure, though, you're not putting me on? I mean, all the trust stuff—it's not just a gimmick?"

"Quite the contrary. Trust can spell the difference between success and failure for your business. Let me put it this way: Success is the result of productivity. Productivity comes from people working *together* to produce quality goods and services. Trust is the glue that binds them together."

Show Your Trust in Employees

"How do you show your trust for your employees, Ted?"

"Give them work that really matters. Encourage them to take risks. Motivate them to find new and better ways of doing the job. Reward right results, not wrong ones. These are just a few of the main incentives."

"One of the things I think I'm hearing, Ted, is that you respect your employees. And in return they respect you."

"And I respect their *potential.* People are not machines to be driven. Old-time managers did this. These days it just won't work."

"But don't we still have a lot of these old-timers around?"

"Their numbers are diminishing, but unfortunately, we still have a lot of *machine thinking* around—managers who divide management into the 'hard' and the 'soft' stuff."

Remember Both the Hard and the Soft Stuff

"What do you mean by 'hard' and 'soft' stuff, Ted?"

"Hard stuff to them means facts, figures, logic, reason, precise analysis and the search for simple, cause-and-effect relationships. The key words are *control, predictability* and *certainty.* Soft stuff focuses on people issues—emotions, feelings, beliefs. This kind of management solves problems by intuition and hunches. It's qualitative, not quantitative."

"The 'hard' manager doesn't like this?"

"Not a bit. It implies unpredictability and uncertainty, loose discipline and lack of organization. It's just too messy."

"But you use the soft approach, Ted."

"Sometimes. I believe an effective manager has to use both. And know the difference. The soft approach is better for most situations."

"Do you mind if I ask you, Ted, whether you have any scientific basis for what you're telling me?"

"Good question. Scientists discovered a long time ago that the world-as-machine model was all wrong. The world is a living organism, not a dead machine. It's energy in different forms. And so are people. They're not objects to be pushed around. They have energy to be developed."

"Scientists also discovered that the world isn't a collection of separate objects, such as atoms or rocks bouncing around and bumping into each other. Everything is related to everything else. And the same is true of business. This means paying close attention to communication and team building."

Building Trust Through Communication and Team Building

The waiter brought in our coffee. Bill took a sip and asked, "Just how do you go about team building at your company?"

"It's really quite simple. We work together in teams, meeting on a regular basis to share what is going on—accomplishments, objectives, facts and figures, goals reached, problems. We get feedback, make suggestions and then correct course, as the sailors say. The building blocks here are mutual trust, openness and respect."

"Sounds like you believe that your organization should fit the people who work for it, rather than the people trying to fit the organization."

"You've got it, Bill. This means, for instance, that job titles change when jobs change. It means building a different type of control based on self-management and trust. We are developing a responsible group of *associates*—a word I prefer over *employees*—who are able to achieve. Or as the Chinese philosopher Lao-Tsu put it: When the best leader's work is done, the people say, 'We did it ourselves.'"

"I know you don't develop self-management just through meetings.' Do you have some specific tools to work with?"

"Yes. As I view it, developing self-management in a business breaks down into four main tasks—tools, as you put it: inspiration, empowerment, rewards and support."

The waiter brought our check. "Can we talk more about these tools next week, Ted? I know I'm going to be applying some of them to my own business."

"Good! Next Wednesday."

Self-Management Tools

1. *Inspire with purpose.* Purpose begins with a mission, one that lets everyone know where they're headed.
2. *Provide power.* Empowerment skills include measuring performance, delegating effectively, making decisions, resolving conflicts, controlling time and stimulating creativity.
3. *Supply rewards.* Rewards are made on the basis of excellent performance with positive results, not on the basis of status, organization, position or any other negative factors.
4. *Offer support.* We motivate with incentives, not manipulation.

2

Setting the Stage for Top Performance

We both decided on the scallops.

"You were talking last week about the four tasks or tools you consider important in developing good self-management," said Bill, unfolding his napkin. "And I remember the first one was *inspiring with purpose.*"

"We all need a sense of purpose. We want desperately to do something that really matters. Work is more than just having a few bucks to add to our wallet. I give my employees—my associates—the opportunity and resources to do meaningful work, and in return they give the company their top performance."

"By top performance, you mean producing quality goods and services?"

"Exactly. You've hit the key words—*producing* and *quality.* Let's start with producing or productivity. So many managers pay scant attention to improving productivity. They take what I call the short view—focusing on the next quarter's bottom line or short-term profits. Instead, they should be taking the long view—developing skilled workers, making long-term investments, building new plants. Strangely, some managers actually *fear* productivity."

"Fear it?"

"They're afraid it will lower quality and mean more forms to fill out, more gimmicks imposed by top management."

"This isn't necessarily so?"

"Not a bit."

"Then what *is* productivity, Ted?"

"I think it's time for me to give you my productivity formula, Bill."

"Go easy. I'm not much for math."

"Don't worry, this is really quite simple:

Input × Activities + Pride = Quality Productivity."

"Doesn't sound too complicated. Could you define what you mean by those four terms—*input, activities, pride* and *quality productivity?*"

"Yes. Input includes labor, capital, materials, energy and support. Activities are tasks and jobs that add value to the inputs, such as taking raw materials and turning them into widgets or taking raw data and turning this into useful information. . . ."

"And pride?"

"This refers to pride in your work, self-assurance and what I call an attitude of productivity."

"And the result is quality productivity?"

"Yes. Quality productivity is the best possible service or product we can provide. This is what we're in business to achieve. My company's output happens to be in the form of books and services. Every person in our company is busy contributing to this output. If they weren't, frankly, they wouldn't be of value to the organization."

"So, it's important to increase quality productivity? How do you do it?"

"Well, we have three options: (1) reduce input while keeping output the same—that is, use fewer resources to provide the same results; (2) squeeze more output from the same input; or (3) do both—reduce input and increase output. All three mean boosting efficiency and effectiveness."

Three Ways To Increase Quality Productivity

1. Reduce input while keeping output the same—that is, use fewer resources to provide the same results.
2. Squeeze more output from the same input.
3. Reduce input *and* increase output.

"Sounds like you mean that to improve quality productivity we've got to work more effectively and work smarter—or both!"

"Both!"

"Now what about the quality component of productivity? Isn't there danger that improving productivity—or increasing production—could *weaken* quality?"

"Actually, the opposite is true. Poor quality is expensive in the long run. If you don't do it right the first time, you'll have lots of problems such as defective products returned, additional resources needed to rework them and more inspections. And there's a psychological cost, too. Workers lose pride in their jobs and in themselves. Self-esteem goes down, along with the company's reputation. And, believe me, regaining lost customers is much tougher than finding new ones. I know."

"I've heard you have a motto in your company: *Sell on quality, not on price.*"

"Yes. I learned in my prior business, Peterson's House of Fudge, which manufactured candy and ice cream, that productivity and quality go hand in hand. You see, we decided to try paying our candy makers a bonus when they went over 20 batches of fudge a day. We did this even though our standards were high, and we were afraid that anything over 20 batches might mean lowering quality."

"It didn't?"

"No! Our candy makers surprised us. They were soon up to 30 and 40 batches a day of equally high-quality fudge, thereby doubling and tripling their earnings!"

"Ted, back to your equation. I know all three elements—input, activities and output—are important, but which do you, as a good manager, focus on?"

"I focus on all three but with a few caveats. In terms of input, occasionally I see my top managers worrying more about resources than results—such as collecting more data, writing more reports and hiring more people without regard to output. Then I remind them that too much emphasis on input over output can do to a business what too much cholesterol does to your body—harden and clog the 'production arteries.'

"In terms of activities, I tell my associates not to get so wrapped up in *what we do* at work that we can't see results. Good (or perhaps bad) examples of this are salespeople who think about *calls* instead of *sales.* Or computer programmers who think about *programming* rather than *producing* useful programs."

"And in terms of output?"

"The manager who focuses on *output* is in the best shape. He's results oriented. But even output can be overstressed, especially if more output is demanded without attention to the input required. *More* results don't guarantee *better* results."

"I've got a lot to think about, Ted. I guess I'm seeing productivity in a new light."

"Just remember, productivity improvement requires developing an attitude. It's not static; it's dynamic—never, ever standing still, always increasing or decreasing."

"And your employees, or associates as you call them, are with you 100 percent?"

"Yes. We push hard to improve our products and services. It takes 100 percent commitment from *everyone.* Some companies go by the old adage 'If it ain't broke, don't fix it.' We say 'If it ain't fixed, it's gonna break.'"

"I like that!"

We picked up our checks.

"Next Wednesday!"

3

Agreeing On a Mission Builds Strength

Bill was waiting for me at the door of the restaurant, obviously eager to talk.

"Ted, I've been thinking about that 100 percent commitment from your associates that we mentioned last week. I'd like to know how to go about achieving it in my company. My printing plant is a little bit more rough and tumble than your business, you know?"

"I firmly believe that *any* business can build this kind of commitment," I replied as the waiter settled us into our corner table. "First, you develop a *sense of direction*. Define exactly where you want your group to go and build the trust to get it there."

"So your employees—I mean, associates—know, understand and support the direction in which they're going?"

"Right. So many organizations don't have a clear sense of direction that is understood by all. A sense of direction—or *mission*, as I like to call it—helps everyone feel secure and confident. And agreement on goals builds a cooperative spirit."

"And just how do you develop a mission?"

"In three steps, Bill: (1) We define it; (2) We get everyone to understand and support it; and (3) We use it to inspire confidence."

Mission in Three Steps

1. Define it.
2. Get everyone to understand and support it.
3. Use it to inspire confidence.

"How do you define the mission?"

"Well, the general mission of every business is the same."

"To make money?"

"Wrong! To produce quality goods and/or services for its customers at a profit. Money is merely the reward.

"Let me be more specific. In defining the word *mission,* we ask three questions: (1) What is our product/service? (2) Who are our customers? (3) What are our values?

"The first question defines our business—books and services; the second defines our market—the entrepreneur; and the third defines what our company stands for—our values. The mission statement my company has operated with for many years is as follows: 'Our company strategy is to use direct response marketing methods to provide proprietary and primarily business-oriented products that satisfy perpetual, recognized or unrecognized, needs and return healthy profits.'"

"You said, Ted, that the next step in developing a mission, after defining it, is to get everyone to support it. How do you do that?"

"Let me put it this way. We promote democracy through a clear sense of mission. Agreement on the part of our associates as to *ends* allows them more freedom concerning *means.* It helps everyone make decisions independently, innovatively and without fear."

"For instance?"

"A customer calls and asks for something no previous customer has ever wanted. What should you do? The answer is not in a manual and your boss is on vacation. Yet you know customer satisfaction is one of your company's high values. So you go ahead and do what is necessary to satisfy the request."

"When we all keep an eye on our company's mission, we enjoy maximum freedom in getting our jobs done. This encourages initiative and responsibility. Our associates are treated as mature, responsible adults. And they respond accordingly."

Inspiring Confidence Through Communication and Involvement

"And the third step you mentioned in developing mission is to inspire confidence?"

"Yes. I try to instill a can-do attitude in all my associates. I want everyone to feel like a winner!"

"How do you go about doing this?"

"Through *communicating* and *involving*. We all communicate openly and freely. This means more than writing a few goals on a sheet of paper and tacking it on the bulletin board. *It's a daily, hands-on job.* We make our company's mission explicit and talk about our values openly. Talking about mission is vital to our company's success."

"And involvement?"

"People support what they help create. Participation promotes commitment. I initially formed a small group of associates to talk about our company's mission. I got some puzzled looks. Many people were hesitant to talk. It took several meetings to overcome the awkwardness. Then, it all began to happen naturally."

"What exactly do you *do* in these meetings?"

"We constantly redefine and refine our mission. We have even developed a set of patterns through which we put new product or service ideas. Our mission is never static. It's easy to lose sight of the big picture when you're immersed in day-to-day details."

"You mean, Ted, you can become *activity oriented* rather than *direction oriented?*"

"Right. So I've used questions such as these at our meetings:

- Have we lost sight of our mission?
- How do our planned new products measure up to our mission?
- What are some ways to better integrate our values into everyone's job?
- Are our customers telling us something new lately, especially about improving products or services? If so, what?
- Should we change our mission? If so, how?"

"What tools do you use besides meetings to communicate with each other and involve everyone?"

"We use bulletin boards, training and orientation sessions, memos, pictures, cartoons and posters. In larger operations, you can use a newsletter. I particularly like to use stories people can relate to, for example, the salesman who went out of his way to satisfy a customer or a rush job completed under a short deadline. We encourage everyone to share stories and ideas."

"Ted, you make it sound so easy."

"Getting your mission across is easier than getting people to identify with it. If a person's job is far removed from the finished product or if it only produces a small part of the finished product, it's more of a challenge. People need to be convinced that everyone is connected and that an individual job contributes to the success of the whole. We stress the team—us over me. But this is after reassuring everyone that their first loyalty is to themselves.

"Another important point I want to make is that my business operates on a financial budget and profit center basis in which each manager creates a budget for his or her department. The goal is to (1) surpass sales and profit budgets and/or (2) reduce costs below budget estimates. By focusing on *both*—namely, increasing sales while maintaining good controls in every department to insure profits—we feel we have everyone in sales, editorial, customer service, administration, accounting and distribution *working together.*"

"You're meeting your goals?"

"Better! The year prior to selling my company we were 50 percent ahead of our projected budget for the first half of the fiscal year. For this achievement, at a special awards ceremony, we presented everyone in the company with a surprise advance on incentive plan bonuses. The response was tremendous, and my associates worked harder than ever to keep up the good work. The same kind of results are happening in my new company, which I started in 1992."

"I notice you use the word *value* a lot, Ted. And I can see that mission and values are closely related."

Values To Encourage

- Striving to be the best you can be
- Getting the details right
- The importance of people
- Superior quality and service
- Listening closely to customers

"Values are an integral part of everyone's job. They contribute to top-notch performance. They generate pride."

"What about the special Employee of the Year Award that I've heard you mention?"

"Once a year all associates on staff vote for the person they think best reflects our company's values. Criteria can include the best active listener, the person whose performance gets the most respect from colleagues, the associate who provides the most effective feedback and help to others, etc. This award is popular because it's employee inspired, not management imposed."

"And one other idea I've heard you speak of, Ted, is the *eagle.*"

"Yes. One of our operating values is that associates, customers and clients are like eagles. They don't flock to us. We have to find them, select them and deal with them *one at a time.* Like the eagle, they all have the capacity to soar to great heights if we can help them. We help customers soar by providing useful business information and tools. And we help our associates by nurturing their growth.

"We give out Eagle awards to our associates whenever we want to recognize someone, for example, as Eagle of the Month, the Quarter or the Year. They complement other team awards.

"And we can't function effectively without the capable help of suppliers such as printers or the magazines in which we advertise. So, when we feel it's earned, we present them with special Eagle awards, too. We've had several suppliers tell us that in all these years in business no customer has ever recognized them in such a way. The result? They work even harder for us!"

Bill looked at his watch as we picked up our checks. "We've run a little over today, Ted, but I've learned a lot. What's on the agenda for next week?"

"We'll talk about contracting for commitment!"

4

Contracting for Commitment

Bill was late.

"Sorry to hold you up, Ted," he said as he hurried in several minutes after noon. "One of our key people was talking to me about leaving, so I pulled out some of the ideas we've been covering—mission, self-esteem, goals and output. Now he's staying!"

"Good! I'm glad our talks have helped, Bill."

"Me, too, because I think maybe I haven't been listening to him—or to others. We're going to start those weekly meetings you suggested. Now what about this contracting for commitment, Ted?"

"In our company, we work with each and every associate to help him or her develop a real sense of personal mission that in turn creates a deep feeling of commitment."

Help Employees Develop a Personal Mission

"How do you do this?"

"First an associate draws up a *personal mission statement,* setting forth his or her job responsibilities. The associate defines the purpose of his or her responsibilities. The associate defines the purpose of his or her position in the company and what tasks are required to achieve that end."

"Does that relate to the company mission statement we talked about last week?"

"Yes, but this is the associate's *personal* statement. It's similar to a job description but focuses primary attention on the end result and secondarily on the process itself."

"Oh, I get it. This way you make each person's job *direction oriented* rather than *activity oriented.*"

"Exactly. That's why we take it a step further and have our associate prepare a *contract for commitment,* which sets forth specific goals and serves both as a planning tool for the associate and a communication tool with his or her manager."

"I gather you find there is a need for *both* a personal mission statement and a contract for commitment?"

"Yes. We find that defining his or her mission clearly and responsibly strengthens our associate's commitment to achieving the goals set forth under his or her contract for commitment."

"Practically speaking, how does an associate go about drawing up a personal mission statement and a contract for commitment?"

"Let's take them one at a time, Bill. First, on a personal mission statement, an associate first lists his or her job duties, those tasks performed for the company on a regular basis."

"Such as?"

"A few examples might be as follows: (1) develop program schedule requirements, (2) maintain up-to-date client files, (3) secure materials and coordinate personnel, (4) develop and write new proposals, (5) design annual budget, (6) plan and coordinate marketing activities."

"And what does your associate do *after* listing his or her job duties?"

"The associate then drafts the personal mission statement itself. Just like the company defines its purpose and direction, the individual defines his or her role in the company and why it exists. It is amazing how many people are confused about why they perform certain tasks and their role in the overall scheme of business."

"Can you give me an example, Ted? I've always taken it for granted that people know basic things such as why their position exists."

"It's like this. Sometimes we see things in pieces instead of as a whole. For instance, I had a secretary once who described her mission as typing, filing and handling my correspondence. These certainly were some of her duties. However, I saw her mission as being much broader. In general, I saw her as a strong assistant whose job was to free up my time of any tasks or duties she could handle herself. Once we communicated about this, it greatly improved our productivity and our working relationship."

"Wow! It sounds so simple!"

"It is, Bill. Sometimes the most important things are very simple."

"Now, what about the contract for commitment, Ted?

The Contract for Commitment Is Specific

"A contract for commitment first sets specific outputs (goals) to be achieved by a certain date. The goals should be clear, understandable, specific, realistic and mutually agreed upon."

"Can you elaborate, Ted?"

"Yes. It might go like this: 'My goal for the period January 1, 19__ through December 31, 19__ is to increase the productivity of my department significantly by enlisting the full participation of all associates. Specifically, we will work together to increase the turnover of Product X from 100 to 200 by July 1, 19__ and from 200 to 300 by December 31, 19__. We will further work together to reduce overhead costs from 14 percent to 11 percent of sales by July 1, 19__ and to 8 percent of sales by December 31, 19__.'

"Next it lists activities and tasks required to produce the desired output. And finally, it lists other inputs required in terms of material, equipment, capital, etc."

"I must say, Ted, that this contract certainly meets the criteria you mentioned; it's clear, understandable, specific and realistic. You said, though, that it also should be mutually agreed upon?"

"Yes. Our associate then discusses this with his or her manager, and if both agree, they then sign it together. The contract for commitment usually evolves from mutual discussions between them. They very likely may consider questions such as the following: How large is the gap between the desired output and the actual output, if any? What obstacles exist? Can they be overcome? If they can, how and when? If not, why not? They may come up with a long list of possible goals, which they'll then hone down to a few important ones while making sure these goals are all consistent and compatible, not at cross purposes."

"For instance?"

"Well, they might come up with these two goals: (1) increase sales orders of new widgets by July 1 and (2) extend production start date for new widgets to July 15, pending achievement of zero defects in prototypes. Trying to achieve both of these goals would undoubtedly mean delayed orders, angry customers and pressure to produce low-quality widgets."

"From all this, I observe that you emphasize both mission and specific goal setting?"

"Yes. We find that drawing up a mission statement and then setting specific goals in a contract for commitment means these goals are far more likely to be achieved. This generates a sense of spirit and commitment."

"What I think I like the most here, Ted, is this idea of mutual agreement."

"Yes. We have found that clear missions and commitment aren't imposed from without: *They're created from within.* We have also discovered several interesting corollaries to this: (1) Goals chosen by our associates have turned out to be far more challenging and productive than any manager would have selected, (2) maximum freedom to develop a contract means maximum commitment to achieving it and (3) giving associates responsibility for setting their own goals builds strong self-management skills. When associates get a chance to decide where they want to go, they'll usually succeed in getting there."

"Would it be possible for me to have samples of a personal mission statement and a contract for commitment so I can modify them for my plant?"

"You're in luck, Bill. I've brought a couple with me today, and they're all yours."

"Thanks. And next week?"

"Keeping score!"

(Sample)

Personal Mission Statement

Name: Jenny Walton Department: Order Processing

Position: Customer Service Rep Reports to: Linda Lowell

Job Duties: *(List those tasks you perform for the company on a regular basis.)*

Check incoming orders.

Return questionable orders with form.

Check customer credit.

Enter code into data base.

Print out labels.

Check and file orders.

Transmit labels to shipping.

Shred orders semiannually.

Personal Mission Statement: *(Review the tasks listed above and consider the purpose of these tasks in relation to your department and the company as a whole. What does your performance of these tasks accomplish for your department? Your company? The company's customers? Your boss? Answer this by writing, in the space below, a brief description of the purpose of your position, the mission in the department or company that you fulfill.)*

My mission in the company is to provide accurate, timely service of customer orders from receipt to shipment. This helps the company stay competitive within the industry by satisfying the customers' needs and reduces costs incurred by returns and/or reshipments caused by error or delays.

Supervisor's Comments:

Jenny's contributions to the dept. and the company have significantly reduced costs while preserving quality. In addition to clearly understanding her mission, Jenny has made numerous suggestions that have been helpful to me, as her supervisor, and to the dept. as a whole.

Signed (Employee) /Date Signed (Supervisor) /Date

Note: *The following page contains a blank form that may be reproduced for your personal use if you wish. Or, you may want to modify it and create your own.*

Personal Mission Statement

Name: ______________________ Department: ____________________
Position: ______________________ Reports to: ____________________

Job Duties: *(List those tasks you perform for the company on a regular basis.)*

____
____
____
____
____
____
____
____

Personal Mission Statement: *(Review the tasks listed above and consider the purpose of these tasks in relation to your department and the company as a whole. What does your performance of these tasks accomplish for your department? Your company? The company's customers? Your boss? Answer this by writing, in the space below, a brief description of the purpose of your position, the mission in the department or company that you fulfill.)*

____
____
____
____
____
____

Supervisor's Comments:

____
____
____
____
____
____

______________________________ ______________________________
Signed (Employee) /Date Signed (Supervisor) /Date

(Sample)

Contract for Commitment

We find that goal setting is a high priority for all of us—a priority that we reevaluate at periodic intervals. We also recognize that manager and managee need to be in complete agreement on goals. This establishes a cooperative, productive workplace, and misunderstandings and communication gaps are minimized when this is accomplished. The contract for commitment that we have drawn up is both a planning tool for the associate filling it out and a communication tool for the manager and associate working together to increase productivity.

Name: Jenny Walton Department: Order Processing
Position: Customer Service Rep Reports to: Linda Lowell

Output for the Period: January 1, 1993 to December 31, 1993

My goal for this period is to increase processing of orders from 10,000 to 13,000 with a turnaround time of one week or less. This would obviate our continuing backlog of approximately 3,000 orders and current turnaround time of two weeks. I am also setting a goal of a maximum of 15 customer complaints due to delay or error on my part, rather than the 42 customer complaints we received during 1992.

Inputs Required: *(Include materials, equipment, support, capital, etc.)*

Computer/printer use—30 hours weekly

Computer paper, stationery, forms and labels

File folders and one additional cabinet

Shredder use—40 hours total

Periodic supervisor consultation to improve technical product knowledge

Rewards Desired:

One complimentary day off for every 1,000 orders processed over 10,000 or payment for additional day if volume requires my presence in the office

Cost: $15,000

Notes:

Signed (Employee) /Date Signed (Supervisor) /Date

Note: *The following page contains a blank form that may be reproduced for your personal use if you wish. Or, you may want to modify it and create your own.*

Contract for Commitment

We find that goal setting is a high priority for all of us—a priority that we reevaluate at periodic intervals. We also recognize that manager and managee need to be in complete agreement on goals. This establishes a cooperative, productive workplace, and misunderstandings and communication gaps are minimized when this is accomplished. The contract for commitment that we have drawn up is both a planning tool for the associate filling it out and a communication tool for the manager and associate working together to increase productivity.

Name: ______________________ Department: ____________________

Position: ____________________ Reports to: ____________________

Output for the period: ____________, 19____ to ____________, 19____

____

____

____

____

____

____

____

____

Inputs Required: *(Include materials, equipment, support, capital, etc.)*

____

____

____

____

____

____

Rewards Desired:

____

____

____

Cost: ______________________

Notes: ____

____

____

______________________________ ______________________________

Signed (Employee) /Date Signed (Supervisor) /Date

(Sample)

Weekly Priority Feedback

Name: ______________________ Week Ending: ____________________

Duty	Quantity Received	Quantity Processed	Total Cumulative
Incoming orders	200	180	(12,820)
Credit checks	180	180	
Database code entry	180	180	
Printing labels	180	180	
Filing	180	180	
Labels to shipping	180	150	
Customer complaints	15	0	

Priorities for Coming Week:

–Remaining duties from above–completion of outstanding order processing

–Responding to customer complaints–will need management assistance with three letters received.

Note: For many positions, it is advisable to *monitor* progress on a weekly basis to measure progress toward goals as outlined on the *contract for commitment.* The above is an example of a report submitted weekly for the position used in this example.

5

Keeping Score

This week *I* was a little late. Bill was waiting.

"I'm ready to hear about keeping score, Ted. You said this was important to productivity."

I smiled. "Very important. Quality productivity is impossible if you can't measure it. My associates and I improve *only if we keep score.*"

"Doesn't this show a lack of trust?"

"No, just the opposite. It *builds* trust. If associates see that no score is being kept, they wonder if the boss really cares about their performance. If not, why trust him? It's like a football game. Imagine a game where no one keeps score and where the field doesn't have any end zones, goalposts or yardage markers. Sounds silly, doesn't it? Why plan?"

"And many companies are like that?"

"Yes. Managers send their 'players' onto the field without any way to keep score. Or if they do keep score, it's used as a *club,* not a *tool.* You know the stereotype—a grim-faced quality control inspector stalking the shop floor, looking over everyone's shoulder and scribbling on a clipboard."

Measuring Output Builds Trust

The waiter brought our veal marsala.

"Let me mention two negative traps managers fall into when they think about keeping score. First, they don't *want* to measure performance because *measurement establishes accountability."*

"Meaning!"

"Anything that can be measured can be evaluated. And most of us would rather avoid evaluation if it means getting criticized. Many managers say, 'You can't measure what I do. No way can you measure judgment or creativity. I'm not a robot.' Of course, this is a cop-out. *Everything* can be measured if you're *willing* to measure it."

"What's the other trap?"

"Managers reward the *wrong output."*

"Because they can't identify it?"

"Not necessarily. Instead, they reward performance that can be measured, rather than performance that *should* be measured."

"For example?"

"They measure *short-term profits* rather than *long-term productivity,* or *paper* production instead of *idea* production. When they do this, they're rewarding short-term thinking and make-work, rather than creativity and innovation. In other words, they're overlooking the very behavior that contributes most to increasing productivity."

"But what about the average worker on, say, the assembly line or in the shipping department?"

"It works there, too—and very well. For instance, a while ago our shipping department was having trouble with boxes being broken and merchandise ruined. Orders were piling up. Rather than lecturing workers or threatening punishments, we instituted a measurement program. Workers were instructed to count the number of broken boxes and the number of orders completed on time. The results were plotted on a large graph displayed where everyone could see it. Within a month, the percentage of broken boxes dropped to almost zero. And the percentage of orders completed on time increased almost 100 percent."

"Isn't this turning people into machines, Ted?"

"Not at all. We don't apply mechanical principles where they *don't* belong—to feelings, beliefs, values, etc. Take our friend Joe, the golfer. You know him, and you've seen all those trophies and momentos he keeps in his den."

"And those computer printouts that list the number of greens hit and the average number of birdies, pars and bogies per round?"

"Right! That way, he says he knows how well he's doing, what part of his game is causing him problems and exactly where to work to improve it."

"I see what you mean, Ted. But do you have any kind of *system* for measuring your workers, rather your associates?"

"Yes. We have a three-part measuring system—one that we feel is simple, yet accurate."

Three-Part Measuring System

1. *Production indicators* define input and output.
2. *Production ratios* compare input and output.
3. *Quality standards* are yardsticks against which to compare productivity changes and to define success.

"Starting with *production indicators,* Ted, how do they *define* input and output?"

"They're like yard markers on the football field. Without them, referees would be forced to pace off every play. Players would get frustrated and fans bored. A business lacking indicators can be just as frustrating. So we take our various departments—personnel, shipping, sales, data processing, etc.—and establish indicators for every aspect of each one."

"For instance?"

"Well, take personnel. We have ten indicators. Five of them are *input indicators*—number of offers, number of interviews, overhead costs, recruiting costs and man-hours worked. Two are *output indicators* (which directly affect output)—absenteeism, turnover rates and number of grievances."

"You use these productivity indicators in all departments?"

"We do. And next week I'll bring you a printout of indicators for all our departments. It may help you create useful score cards for your plant."

"Thanks, Ted. I know it will."

"Moreover, we make *everyone* responsible for *helping develop their own indicators.* This gets people to focus objectively on what they do."

"This really works?"

"With remarkable results. Our publishing division, for instance, came up with these indicators: number of books published per year, number of books sold per year, number of sales generated by the books and number of sales per advertising dollar spent. They also came up with a card deck to advertise our products to our clients. Since other advertisers can also advertise in the card deck, the number of new and existing clients who advertise is another indicator. Our company operates with a number of profit centers, so we look at indicators that measure how close we come to sales and profit projections and how well we keep costs down."

"You said that your second type of measure is *productivity ratios.*"

"Yes. Productivity ratios are output indicators over input indicators. We use three ratios: (1) *company ratios,* (2) *group ratios* and (3) *individual ratios.*

"There are many useful company ratios. Some organizations use financial indicators, such as profitability and price recovery. We also use these ratios regularly, but since many associates do not control them directly, I'd rather talk about group and individual ratios today."

"Such as?"

"Perhaps the most relevant group ratio is *labor productivity*—how well our associates use their time and energy. Labor productivity equals the total number of output units divided by the total of man-hours worked. And we break this down further into *direct labor productivity* and *indirect labor productivity.* If your company is manufacturing widgets, for example, direct labor productivity equals the total number of widgets divided by the total of man-hours worked, while indirect labor productivity equals the total number of new accounts divided by the total number of man-hours."

"Then what are individual ratios, Ted?"

"Individual ratios are basically the same as group ratios—units of output divided by number of man-hours. For example, an editor working alone can measure her personal output by the number of pages edited. But a group designing a budget produces a group output. We save time and energy, however, by using individual ratios only when individual output is obvious. Otherwise we use group or departmental ratios."

"We've talked about production indicators and productivity ratios. Now, what about the third type of measurement—quality standards?"

"It's perhaps the most important measure, Bill. As I said before, a lot of managers claim the more significant aspects of their jobs, such as motivating people and making complicated decisions, can't be measured—that quality is subjective and can't be evaluated."

"You don't agree?"

"No. Quality *can* and *must* be measured."

"How?"

"Quality standards begin as abstract words, such as effectiveness, quality or reliability. The next step is to translate them into specific terms.

"Take 'quality' for example. The typist can measure quality by looking at the number of errors in each letter. The salesperson might define quality by the total dollar value of his or her orders. Or the shipping department defines quality by the number of orders sent out correctly or the percentage of breakage. These are *direct* measurements. Some aspects of work, such as *employment morale,* for example, have to be measured *indirectly.* However, while there's no direct measure for this, we can look at absenteeism rates, turnover rates and the number of employee grievances. Taken together, these indicators give us a rough indication of morale."

"You've talked about measuring quality, indicating there are standards for successful performance."

"Right, Bill. The standard is the goal you want to shoot for. With the typist, it might be zero errors per letter, or for the order processing department, it might be zero mistakes per order. And we've found that *graphing* measurements is a powerful way to present data."

"You mean 'One picture is worth a thousand words.'?"

"Yes. Graphs are a great way to identify relationships and trends. They help uncover important information—e.g., comparing the number of sales calls to the number of new accounts generated by a salesperson. They can also point up interesting relationships—e.g., in March and June, when the number of sales calls is highest, new orders are lowest."

"I'd like to give this a try at our plant, Ted."

"You'll be surprised at the results, Bill. Next week I'll bring you a copy of our measurement checklist. Right now I'll just mention six measurement criteria we use. They are as follows:

1. Are we measuring the right output?
2. Are the indicators precise?
3. Is the measurement complete?
4. Is the measurement available in real time?
5. Were the measurements developed by the persons using them?
6. Can everyone understand them?"

"Developing a good measurement system takes a lot of time, doesn't it, Ted?"

"Yes. And it's not easy. It doesn't happen overnight, and maintaining it costs money. That's the reason many companies don't bother with it at all. They practice what I call 'productivity through hope.' This means coasting along and waiting for magic to improve things."

"I'm afraid I've been guilty of that, Ted!"

"Other companies practice 'productivity by decree.' They *demand* productivity and punish people if they don't get it. Neither system works well. *A truly successful business keeps score.* The better our score keeping, the better our results!"

"This has been a good session for me, Ted. What's on the menu for next week?"

"How about *sharing positive power?*"

"Sounds great! See you next Wednesday."

Productivity Indicators To Keep Score

(as discussed in this chapter)

I = Input indicators
O = Output indicators
Unlabeled—indicators indirectly affecting output

Administration:
- Number of letters typed (O)
- Number of errors per letter (O)
- Number of copies made (O)
- Number of phone calls answered (I)
- Number of orders processed (O)
- Cost of supplies ordered (I)
- Number of orders received (I)

Data Processing:
- Number of lines of code per program (O)
- Orders processed (O)
- Processing time/minutes (I)
- Number of new programs developed (O)
- Data processing expenses (I)

Maintenance:
- Square feet cleaned (O)
- Maintenance expenses (I)
- Man-hours worked (I)

Marketing:
- Market share (O)
- Promotion and advertising expenses (I)
- Number of contacts made (I)

Quality Control:
- Number of defects/units
- Number of units returned
- Reworking time/man-hours (I)

Sales:
- Number of sales calls made (I)
- Number of units sold (O)
- Dollar value of sales (O)
- Number of new accounts opened (O)
- Overhead expenses (I)
- Salesperson turnover

Measurement Checklist

(as discussed in this chapter)

1. *Does your productivity indicator measure the right output?*

A useful productivity ratio must include the right output. A salesperson's output is *not* the number of sales calls he or she makes. These are activities. The output is *new accounts opened or sales made.* A personnel manager's output is not the number of interviews but the *number of persons hired.*

Activities are often more visible and more tangible than output, so it's tempting to substitute them for output. Don't! Encourage your associates to concentrate on output, not "producing" activities. Remember, you're in business to produce *quality output,* not activities.

2. *Are the indicators precise?*

It's easy to choose the wrong unit of measurement. For example, an inventory clerk's job is to fill orders. Is the *number of orders filled* the right indicator? No. Each order is different. Some contain a single item while others contain dozens. The current unit of measurement is the *number of items pulled.*

A proposal writer's output isn't the number of proposals written. Each proposal is different. So to develop useful measurements, proposals must be broken down—by number and type of sections or by some other indication of the job's complexity.

Precision also means identifying the *exact source of labor.* If your proposal writer required 20 hours less to produce a proposal in May than in April, you might be tempted to celebrate. But if he or she used 40 hours of his or her assistant's time for research, productivity actually decreased.

3. *Is the measurement complete?*

A good measurement system takes into account all relevant inputs. A common example is labor cost. If your associates produce 50 percent more output in period B than in period A, you might conclude that productivity rose. But if labor costs rose 75 percent during the same period, total productivity *per labor dollar* actually went down.

4. *Is the measurement available in real time?*

Feedback is useful when it's available. Continuous feedback helps our associates solve problems in time to make a difference. As one football coach commented, "If you have something useful to tell me, let me know on Saturday afternoon, not Monday morning."

Individual or group measures are useful when they are reported every week or every month. Departmental or divisional measures are more general; they can be reported monthly or quarterly. And companywide measures are probably most useful when reported semiannually or annually.

5. *Were the measurements developed by the people using them?*

   The people using the measurement should develop them. Designing a measurement system helps workers distinguish between input, activities and output. And participation decreases *fear of measurement* and increases *commitment.*

6. *Can everyone understand them?*

   A good system is simple but not simplistic. Complicated and confusing measurements are worse than worthless because what people don't understand they fear. It can be to your advantage to hire a consultant to come in for a couple of days and teach everyone the fundamentals of your measurement system. If forced to choose between a perfect system that only a few managers can understand and a cruder system that everyone can understand, opt for the latter.

6

Sharing Positive Power

Again, Bill was waiting.

"Good news?" I asked.

"Yes," he replied. "I had a meeting with my managers Monday about the quality standards and performance measurement we talked about last week. They feel, as I do, that developing a good measuring system is something we have needed in our company for a long time."

"Good!"

"But how about this 'positive power' you said we'd be discussing today, Ted? Is this related to the positive thinking we used to hear so much about?"

I smiled. "In a way. You see, when you share power in a group, you build trust. And the more power a group has, the more it accomplishes."

"But doesn't that mean giving up control?"

"In a sense, but the key word here is *share.* Unless you give your associates power, they can't produce. They can't turn inputs into outputs. Their untapped potential goes to waste. Empowering your associates means doing everything you can to help them become ready, willing and able to do the best possible job."

"I guess I have a little trouble, Ted, with the word *power.* It conjures up some negative thoughts, like *abuse of power, power-hungry* or people on a *power trip.*"

"Abusing power or using it to coerce *is* negative, but power is a neutral word. It comes from the Greek *poters,* meaning 'to be able to.' Thus, a person with power is able to *do* something—produce, influence events and people and come up with results. Empowering your associates is enabling them."

"I see. And just *how* do you go about giving your associates power, Ted?"

"You follow these four steps: (1) assign responsibility, (2) grant authority, (3) supply resources and (4) remove obstacles.

Four Steps of Empowerment

1. Assign responsibility.
2. Grant authority.
3. Supply resources.
4. Remove obstacles.

"How do you assign responsibility?"

"I view responsibilities, Bill, as tasks or duties my associate agrees to perform. They are *accounts.* And accountability means my associate's willingness to answer for the results—good or bad. When responsibility is clear, we know who to hold accountable when things go wrong or who to praise when things go right."

"And your second step? How do you grant authority?"

"Authority means the right to command or decide. A person with authority has *permission* to act. In an organization where power is centralized, rather than delegated, a few people at the top give orders and everyone else follows them. The top bosses decide and the rest carry out their decisions. In a democratic organization, authority is widely distributed. All our associates have the authority to make certain decisions."

"For instance?"

"Take our display manager. She sets up our book displays. You've seen them."

"They're real eye-catchers, Ted!"

"That's it, Bill. She has a flair for catching the eye of potential purchasers. We virtually give her a free hand at doing this, not only at our company but also with bookstores and other retail outlets."

"As for your third step, how do you supply resources?"

"By way of illustration, our editorial manager is given the necessary staff, equipment and time to do her job effectively so that she can meet her output goals."

"And your fourth step was to remove obstacles?"

"Yes. The editorial manager I just mentioned could not do her job with authors interfering, so we grant her total authority for making editorial changes and decisions."

Power Must Be Positive

"Then positive power means sharing responsibility, authority and resources?"

"Right. Power isn't a pie that my associates try to cut in order to get the biggest slice for themselves and leave the crumbs for someone else. Instead, we ask whether everyone has enough responsibility, authority and resources to do the best possible job. We put it this way:

- Is everyone *responsible* for producing some output?
- Does everyone have the *authority* to make the decisions necessary to carry out this responsibility?
- Does everyone have the *resources* necessary to produce results?"

"Then you're really talking about *delegating* responsibility?"

"Yes. But at this point I'd like to compare *positive* versus *negative* power to clear up some misconceptions a lot of people have. Let me get negative power out of the way first. Negative power exists when the responsibility, authority and resources are withheld or are 'out of sync.' Responsibilities in this kind of company are not clearly defined, and authority is lacking or abused. An example is the engineer who controls a machine worth $10 million but doesn't have the clout to order $50 worth of supplies without filling out a dozen forms, which all have to be approved by someone else. Or there's the manager who uses his authority to hire and fire as a stick to instill fear and coerce desired behavior."

"And this destroys trust?"

"Absolutely! And it lowers productivity. Workers spend most of their time trying to please the boss instead of increasing production. Or they may just rebel, and then *nothing* gets done!"

"So, instead, managers should be delegating?"

"Yes. That's positive power. It's power based on 'followership.' A manager *earns leadership power* by proving he is worth following. The late William Gore of W.L. Gore & Associates called it 'natural leadership defined by followership.'"

"That way you build a stronger *team*?"

"Right. Delegating wisely builds a strong business team because it builds trust. And an important point I want to make is that our managers delegate responsibility and authority, but we *retain accountability.* We don't keep looking over our associates' shoulders as they work, but we do monitor their output so we know whether they're doing their jobs!"

"As I tell my managers, 'Because you're accountable for the results, you're responsible for measuring them, and for helping and supervising your associates. If you don't accept this responsibility, then you're passing the buck!"

"Do you have some criteria for delegating, Ted?"

Three Criteria for Delegating

1. Define Output.
2. Provide Training.
3. Recognize Complexity of Task.

"Yes. I have three basic criteria: (1) *What's the required output?* (2) *Does the associate have enough skill to accomplish the task?* (3) *Am I really aware of the complexity of the task?* If my associate doesn't have the necessary skills to do the job, we may have to invest in education and training, or balance the costs of training against the benefits of delegating. And understanding the associate's job is equally important because nothing is more frustrating than getting feedback from a boss who doesn't recognize the difficulty of the tasks he is delegating."

"I've had that happen, Ted!"

"I have, too. Once I had a boss who had no idea how time-consuming writing is. Because he wasn't a writer himself, he couldn't understand why it took me so long to turn his jumbled facts and semicoherent thoughts into clear, well-organized reports."

"Do you delegate all the way from top to bottom, so to speak?"

"We do, at least to the lowest level likely to produce a quality decision. Who should make a decision depends on the type of decision being made. *Policy* decisions are best delegated to top managers and *operating* decisions to operating personnel or first-line supervisors. We always ask this question: Is this decision consistent with our associate's output responsibility?"

"I suspect you have guidelines on this, Ted?"

"You guessed it. In fact, there are three guidelines:

1. Delegate to the person who has the best facts or can get them most easily.
2. When facts come from different sources, delegate to the person skilled at integrating them, the one with enough experience to evaluate the big picture.
3. Delegate to the person who is in the best position to make the decision by a certain time."

"In spite of what you say, Ted, aren't there dangers to be wary of in delegating?"

"There are. For instance, some managers delegate tasks they know should be delegated, but they'd really rather do the tasks themselves. For example, the manager will ask an associate to write a report. Then when the first draft arrives on the manager's desk, he or she will edit, inject new ideas, make extensive changes and send it on to the word processing department. The associate gets no feedback at all! Is this sincere delegation? Hardly. I'd call it *partial delegation* at best."

"In other words, if a manager thinks he can do everything better than anyone else, why hire anyone else?"

"Right. Managers so often don't delegate because they lack confidence in their associates' abilities and seriously underestimate their potential. They rationalize this mistrust by claiming they can do the job better themselves. Or they claim they *prefer* to do it themselves."

"And that breeds more mistrust?"

"Yes. When a manager fails to delegate, no one else learns how to do the job. Inexperience breeds still more mistrust. You think your associates can't do it, so *you* have to do it!"

"But what about people who *don't want* responsibility? Do you fire them?"

"Firing, we find, is seldom a good answer. Instead, we realize that reluctance to accept a delegated task may stem from the fact that an associate is unwilling to take a risk, is afraid of criticism, lacks confidence or doesn't have the proper resources to do the job."

"What do you do in these situations?"

"Well, we know that much of this is caused by managers who lack confidence in their associates, so their associates lack confidence in themselves. Breaking this cycle means taking a risk. And, we make it a calculated risk by doing just the things we've been talking about today. To recap, we define output clearly, offer education and training as necessary, delegate decisions to the proper level and monitor and supervise output carefully."

"It certainly seems to work for you, so it should work for us, Ted."

"It will, Bill. I guarantee it. Effective delegation builds a powerful team, and powerful followers make powerful leaders."

"What's in store for next week?" Bill asked as we picked up our checks.

"Let's try talking about open and honest communication."

"Good."

7

How Active Is Your Listening?

We arrived at the restaurant door simultaneously and went right to our corner table.

"Ted, are we going to talk today about communicating openly and honestly?"

"Right. We get things done only when we communicate effectively with each other. Conversely, when projects and schedules start slipping, it's usually because our channels of communication are *not* working and our signals are getting crossed. Our associates begin to feel defensive and suspicious, so trust flies out the window."

"What do you do when this happens?"

"We remind ourselves that *quality communication* is a top priority for all of us. We talk about it and we work at bringing it about."

Quality Communication Builds Trust

"How do you define quality communication, Ted?"

"Quality communication is honest. It contributes to building mutual trust, and it results in accurate exchanges of information.

"Let's start with the idea of honesty. Some managers manipulate information deliberately to promote their own interests. Of course, what they really promote is distrust and suspicion."

"And they thereby destroy their credibility?"

"Yes, Bill. Honesty and credibility, or trust, go hand in hand. In fact, I've found that where there's trust, even clumsy messages get through."

"You said that quality communication results in *accurate* exchanges of information. Can you elaborate?"

"Let's look at communication as a transaction. The four variables of the transaction in sequence are sender, message, receiver and feedback."

"And feedback is the most important?"

"Absolutely, Bill. There's no real communication until the listener understands the message, accepts it and lets the sender know he or she understands it. You've heard the story about the tree falling in the forest? If no one is around, has the tree made a sound? Physically, yes. There are sound waves, but there's really no sound unless someone hears it."

"I see what you mean. But practically speaking, how do you actually develop good communication?"

"First let me tell you what we've discovered does *not* work. And then I'll go on to what, through trial and error, we've discovered *does* work."

Obstacles to Quality Communication

1. Words
2. Context
3. Filtering
4. Wrong assumptions

"We've found there are four major obstacles to quality communication. First are the tools we use—*words.* Words can confuse.

Even simple words and phrases can convey different meanings. The 500 most common words in the English language have 14,070 meanings. No wonder it's tough getting things across! And the same words and gestures used by different cultures can cause even more problems. Words also have different connotations. I mentioned this several weeks ago in connection with the word power, which can be a positive, negative or neutral word."

"And the second obstacle?"

"*Context.* Meaning depends on context. Fifty degrees and warm is beautiful weather in November in Chicago, but in Hawaii it's a disaster. Context can also be affected by personal history, professional background or specific circumstances."

"Could you give me an example, Ted?"

"Sure. A farmer was watching a painter sit before his easel. 'You're resting,' the farmer said. 'No,' the painter replied, 'I'm working.' Later the farmer passed the painter's home, where the painter was digging in his garden. 'Ah, now you're working,' the farmer said. 'No, now I'm resting from my work,' replied the painter."

"I see, Ted. Context helps create meaning. And it also can create misunderstanding?"

"Yes. And sometimes context is more important than content. For example, a manager says to a promotional director, 'Hey, Dave. How did it go with those brochures?' And Dave responds, 'No problems, Betty. They're going out tomorrow.'

"But another dialogue might run as follows: The manager says, 'Hey, Dave. How did it go with those brochures?' And Dave replies, 'Well, that damn printer finally got his act together and sent them over. They're going out tomorrow.'

"The content is the same in both cases. The brochures are finished and ready to mail. But the emotional messages are quite different. The wise manager responds to the emotional context, not just the content. He or she must be sensitive to what's going on beneath the surface."

"What's the third obstacle to quality communication?"

"*Filtering,* Bill. In many companies there are lots of people between the message senders and the intended recipients. Everyone filters a little before sending on a message."

"You mean if the boss wants to hear good news, the bad parts are filtered out?"

"Exactly. Or if a mistake is made, the message is changed to disguise it."

"And what is the fourth obstacle to good communication?"

"*Wrong assumptions.*"

"Which means?"

"Assumptions control how we interpret messages. They are statements about the world that we accept without proof. Everyone has hundreds of assumptions. We'd go crazy without them. Imagine *not* assuming the sun will rise tomorrow. Everything is interpreted by us in the light of our own personal assumptions. Confusion comes when people bring different assumptions to the same message."

"I'm sure you can give me an example, Ted."

"Let's say you decide to start a productivity program in your printing plant. You distribute a memo, saying 'In response to our concern about lower productivity, the division chiefs have decided to implement a productivity program. Improving productivity over the next quarter will become our highest priority.' Reactions to this memo will vary with assumptions about productivity."

"You mean the person who assumes that increasing productivity means *working harder* will think 'Nuts, I'll probably have to come in on Saturdays'?"

"Right. And the person who assumes that increasing productivity means *working smarter* will think, 'Great. Now my department will get some help for once. I'd love to see my associates getting things done on time.' But now let's move on to the positive—what do we do to achieve real quality communication."

"I'm listening, Ted."

"There, you've got it, Bill! *Active listening* is the key to successful communication. If you listen actively, you can overcome all the obstacles we've talked about."

"What do you mean by *honest attention,* Ted?"

"I mean really hearing what's being said. If you can't hear, move closer or ask the person to speak up. Avoid interrupting the speaker. Use eye contact and appropriate body language. Leaning away from the person communicates indifference. Leaning slightly forward conveys interest. Encourage people to talk with phrases such as 'Tell me more,' 'Maybe I can help' or 'I'd like to know more about that.'"

How To Listen Actively

1. Give your honest attention.
2. Clarify messages.
3. Reflect understanding back to the sender.
4. Make implicit assumptions explicit.
5. Listen for intellectual and emotional content.
6. Avoid criticizing, evaluating or judging.
7. Encourage associates to take responsibility to solve their own problems.

"Please explain *clarifying messages.*"

"Ambiguous and confusing messages should be clarified. Translate them into specific, concrete terms. For example, one manager says, 'I'd like a report on Division One's productivity for the past two quarters.' And his associate responds, 'I'm not sure I know what kind of productivity you want to analyze.' The manager replies, 'I want some indication of indirect labor costs in that area.' So the associate clarifies, 'You're looking then for an indirect labor-output ratio with cost increases factored out?' And the manager confirms, 'That's it.'"

"Next, you mentioned *reflecting understanding back to the sender.*"

"That means restating what you've heard in your own words. If you don't have enough facts, get more. Ask questions, starting with *what, where, when* and *why.* Above all, avoid jargon, technical or otherwise."

"What do you mean by *make implicit assumptions explicit?*"

"If you feel incorrect assumptions are causing misunderstanding, put them into words. Talk about them. For example, one manager says, 'We have to take a closer look at the production department. They're making only 60 percent of their deadlines. Editorial is making 85 percent.' His or her associate asks, 'Are you assuming they get a comparable amount of time?' The manager responds, 'Don't they?' The associate replies, 'Not by a long shot. Editorial has twice as much time as production.' You see, assumptions are difficult to recognize. They're what people are *not* saying. It takes careful listening and probing to uncover them."

"You said, Ted, that another component of active listening is *listening for intellectual and emotional content?"*

"Yes. Most messages contain both, but often the emotional is more important. Look for nonverbal cues that express emotion when words and tone of voice don't. What is the *underlying* message? It may be a call for help or an emotion the speaker hesitates to express openly. You can use phrases such as 'Are you feeling . . . ?' or 'I was feeling you might be . . . .' Try not to exaggerate or minimize the other person's feelings. Just take your time as you probe for the real message."

"You also cautioned against *criticizing, evaluating* or *judging."*

"I did. Evaluation so often takes place too early or inappropriately. It's frequently seen as a threat and causes defensiveness. So try to keep an open mind. Only in an atmosphere of trust and respect will people consider different points of view."

"I can see that judging and criticizing can be roadblocks to real empathy."

"They are. And so are commanding, threatening, moralizing and arguing."

"Then you advise that as an employer I concentrate on praising, reassuring and making suggestions to my associates?"

"As long as your suggestions and reassurance don't make your associates helpless and incapable of solving their own problems. Timing is important. Too often listeners step in to solve a problem before they understand it. Active listening, effectively practiced, *helps people assume responsibility for solving their own problems.* It encourages autonomy and better self-management."

"Then I guess the primary goal of active listening is empathy and the secondary goal is self-management?"

"Well put, Bill," I replied glancing at my watch. "I see we have talked a little longer than usual today, but perhaps we could sum it up by saying that as an active listener, stop thinking *about* or *for* people and starting thinking *with* people."

8

Diffusing Our Differences

"You didn't tell me last week, Ted, what our topic would be today."

"How about *turning conflict into cooperation?*"

"Sounds good to me. We have had a couple of disagreements at the plant this week that I'd like to resolve. So maybe you can give me some pointers."

"Glad to. And rest assured you're not unique. Conflict happens every day in every business! A manager wants the new warehouse located near the corporate offices, while her colleague emphatically insists it should be near the manufacturing plant. Or a supervisor wants to fire a worker for alleged insubordination, but his boss likes the worker and wants to keep her."

"Sounds a lot like our place, Ted!"

Conflict Can Be Healthy

"Let's distinguish here between *healthy* conflict or honest disagreement, which is normal, and *unhealthy* conflict, which is disruptive. The latter can lower productivity, drain energy from the job at hand and turn the workplace into a battleground."

"And destroy the kind of trust we've been talking about building?"

"Right. In an environment filled with unhealthy conflict everyone lives in fear of attack. They suspect their colleagues are out to get them. So, rather than cooperate, they defend and counterattack."

"But you endorse healthy conflict, Ted?"

"Emphatically. Healthy conflict is an integral part of *growth,* both personal and professional, and it's inevitable in any dynamic group. By avoiding conflict, we often inhibit creativity. And without creativity, we limit growth severely."

"But I've always thought a good manager avoided disagreements, tried to smooth over differences and kept the boat from rocking."

"Sweeping conflict under the rug doesn't get rid of it, Bill. It just turns it into resistance or resentment. Then morale takes a nose dive, and so does productivity."

"I guess that figuring out *why* we have unhealthy conflicts might help us determine how to solve them."

"Right. Some people point to personality clashes as the source of conflicts. Joan's aggressive manner clashes with Bob's laid-back style. Or Joe can't stop arguing, so he's always in trouble with his co-workers."

"But you don't buy this, Ted?"

"Not really. It hasn't helped me solve any conflicts. I find it more useful to look at *needs* and *resources.*"

Meet Specific Needs by Allocating Resources

"We all have *basic needs:* security, money, recognition, fulfillment and control over our lives. But we also have *specific needs* in *specific situations.* For example, Kathy needs a bigger office in which to hold staff meetings, John needs a new computer to keep up with his workload or Dave needs approval for a new project."

"And how do we meet these needs, Ted?"

"With physical resources such as materials, equipment and energy. Or interpersonal resources such as approval from the boss, respect from peers or compliments from customers. You'll find unfulfilled needs lie at the root of most conflicts. One guy has something; the next guy doesn't. Both want it. Or two workers want their boss's approval, and one of them thinks she's gotten the short end of the stick."

"So what do you do, Ted, when this happens?"

"I ask myself two questions: (1) What do the parties think they need? and (2) What resources are they fighting about?"

"I notice you say *think they need.*"

"Yes. Perception is everything. A person may not actually *need* something, but when the person thinks he or she does and doesn't get it, a conflict arises."

"Once you've acknowledged a conflict exists, what do you do to resolve it?"

"There are basically two ways to settle differences, Bill. I call them *win-lose* or *win-win.*"

Seek Win-Win Solutions

"Too many people think that business is war or that for every winner there's got to be a loser. If *I* win, then you've got to lose. And if *you* win, then I've got to lose."

"So either way there's a loser?"

"Yes, Bill. But luckily there's another alternative. Win-win means *everyone* can be a winner. There's no need for any losers! It means that both sides can have their needs met and that there are plenty of resources to go around. And because conflicts are problems to be solved—not battles to be won—they're resolved through cooperation, consensus and compromise, not by force."

"So how we *look at* conflicts, Ted, determines how we resolve them?"

"Yes. The 'I win–you lose' style is basically aggressive, while the 'I lose–you win' style is basically passive. But the 'I win–you win' style is happily assertive."

"You mean aggressive people want to win even if the victory comes at someone else's expense?"

"Yes. Aggressive people tend to see things in either-or terms. They manipulate, forcing their opponents to *submit* through pressure, threats or confrontation. *Theirs* is the only right solution; everyone else is wrong. Believing his or her solution must be the wrong one, the passive person agrees, and resolves conflicts by giving in. But the assertive person is flexible and realizes that there is more than one right solution, that choices are usually more complicated than 'either-or.' Assertive people aren't critical or judgmental. For them, resolving conflicts is based on *mutual respect* for the needs of both sides."

"Ted, can you tell me step-by-step just how I'd go about achieving a win-win solution?"

"There are four basic steps: (1) establish a trusting relationship; (2) address the problem in terms of needs and interests, not specific position; (3) help others generate alternatives that satisfy everyone and (4) based your decisions on an objective standard."

Four Steps to Win-Win

1. Establish a trusting relationship.
2. Address the problem in terms of needs and interests.
3. Help others generate alternatives that satisfy everyone.
4. Base decisions on an objective standard.

"I can see, Ted, that the initial step, establishing a trusting relationship, is an important one."

"Yes. When a conflict comes to a head, fear and suspicion are usually running rampant on both sides. The conflict is all wrapped up in feelings and emotions. I acknowledge those feelings but try to distinguish them from the conflict itself. That is, I focus on the *deed,* not the *doer,* making certain both sides realize *they're* not the problem. The active listening we talked about last week is important here. It gives people a chance to let off steam."

"Can you give an example, Ted?"

"Let's take our accounting department. Peggy says, 'I can't take this any longer. Either she goes or I go.' Her supervisor responds, 'You sound terribly angry about this situation.' 'You bet I am,' Peggy replies. 'I've had to deal with Barb's screwups all week. She's the reason we're going to miss the March budget deadlines.' Her supervisor asks, 'You're afraid you're not going to make them?' 'We won't without bringing in an experienced temp,' Peggy replies. 'You're considering outside help?' the supervisor asks. And Peggy responds, 'If you and Mr. Brown could approve it first.' Thus, by using active listening this supervisor acknowledged Peggy's anger and let her know it's okay to be angry."

"I see."

"In addition, we try to use I messages instead of you messages. 'You should' or 'your problem is . . .' produce a defensive attitude and only perpetuate the conflict. I messages are nonjudgmental, describe your feelings about the behavior involved and/or give a description of the consequences you perceive."

"For instance, Ted?"

"Here are examples of good I messages: 'Jim, I notice you didn't sign up for the last four projects available.' Or 'Betty, I notice you've been coming in late two or three times a week lately.'"

"The second step is focusing on underlying needs, rather than specific positions?"

"Right. So often conflicts lead to stalemates when both sides dig in. For example, Jack asks Mary, 'How's the budget coming?' Mary emphasizes, 'I need at least two months to get it ready.' Then Jack digs in with 'It's got to be done in a month.' So Mary digs in then and says 'I just can't do it in one month, and that's that.' Result: A stalemate.

"This is a better way to handle it, Bill. When Mary asks for two months, no less, Jack responds, 'You sound really concerned about finishing it.' Mary then says, 'You bet. After the last one, my staff got together and decided we needed two months to do it right.' And Jack replies, 'It sounds like you really want the chairman to know you're doing a good job.' Mary says, 'That's right,' and Jack acknowledges, 'So basically you want to produce a good budget.' You see, Jack has used active listening to uncover the basic need—recognition."

"What about the third step, generating alternatives?"

"Conflicts, Bill, are not necessarily either-or situations. There are usually a number of possible solutions, and some, of course, are compromises. In the situation we just talked about, Jack and Mary compromised on a month and a half to complete the budget. Alternatively, they might have asked for an extension of the budget deadline or called in more help to finish it sooner. If you build a *trusting atmosphere,* then both sides will be motivated to search for the best alternatives."

"And what about the fourth step, basing your decisions on an objective standard?"

"Even when you generate a lot of alternatives, it may not be clear which one is best, so you look for an objective standard. In the case of Mary and Jack, a standard could be a period of time previously allotted to prepare the budget. Or it could be a comparison with other departmental budgets. Objective standards, in general, can include traditional methods, professional standards, budget/cost limitations or comparisons with other companies."

"It appears to me as though your win-win approach in dealing with conflicts is a sure way to develop trust."

"It is, Bill, and knowing that everyone in a group is working to help everyone else satisfy their needs builds security and confidence."

"I've got a lot to think about this week, Ted. And I believe it's going to help me with those disagreements at the plant that I mentioned earlier."

"Good. Then maybe next week we can talk about *participation."*

9

Participation

Bill was waiting eagerly at the door of the restaurant.

"It worked, Ted," he exclaimed, clapping my shoulder. "The win-win approach we talked about last week really worked. You remember those two disagreements I mentioned we were having at the plant? Well, I applied the win-win strategy, and we all came up winners!"

"I'm glad. Shall we go for the shad roe today?"

"Good idea. As I remember, we are going to talk about *participation* today."

"Right. I also call it *building a strong business team.*"

"How do you build this team, Ted?"

"First, we encourage *everyone* to participate insofar as possible in the decision-making process."

"How do you do that?"

"By providing information and ideas, recommending decisions, confirming decisions through consensus and vetoing decisions made by an individual."

"This works?"

"It does! We have found that participation produces *quality* decisions and solutions. It also produces deeper commitment on the part of our associates. Involvement in *making* a decision strengthens their commitment to *implementing* it. Associates feel they own what they have a hand in creating."

"And this builds trust?"

"Yes. If you exclude your workers from effective participation in the decision-making and problem-solving process, they won't feel trusted or respected. They'll just feel powerless."

"I notice you say *effective* participation."

"I use that word because just any kind of participation won't work. It has to be the *right* kind, and you have to guide and facilitate it carefully to make it work. It's a slow day-by-day process that gets easier all the time but still takes a lot of effort and attention."

"Have you measured the effect of participation on your productivity, Ted?"

"Good question. We have, and the effect is strongly positive. As you know, the line between office and factory work is fast blurring these days because computers are turning everyone into thinkers. Former line workers are learning how to program and use computers, and clerical workers are becoming knowledgeable workers."

"So there's actually a lot of brainpower waiting to be tapped?"

"Yes, and participation is a good way to tap it. Japanese managers have long recognized that their employees know the business best and that innovation and improvement must come from the workers."

"Is there a participation process, Ted—that is, steps you take to make it happen?"

"Yes. There are three basic steps: (1) *define output,* (2) *determine who should participate* and (3) *decide how much participation is desirable.*"

"How do you define output?"

"A good output definition tells you the nature of your product or what services you plan to render, such as computerizing your inventory system or investing in Project X or Project Y. It also tells you *when* your output must be produced, *when* operating problems have to be solved and *what decisions* have to be made. A decision made before it's possible to act on it is premature. A decision made too late to act on is worthless. And finally, you need to know *who* will ratify the decision and *who* can veto it."

Three Steps to Effective Participation

1. Define output.
2. Determine who should participate.
3. Decide how much participation is desirable.

"As for the second step, Ted, how do you determine who should participate?"

"The answer to that depends on two other questions: (1) What's the output? and (2) Who's responsible for doing something with it? For example, a decision to buy a new machine should enlist output from its future operator. A decision to go into a new business should be made by top management with input from anyone who has a stake in the outcome. That's why I, or my fellow managers, often participate in lower-level meetings so we can offer suggestions to associates new to, or less familiar with, the problems being addressed."

"Can you explain the third step, decide how much participation is desirable?"

"This is a question that baffles many managers. Everyone should participate as much as possible, and anyone who has the opportunity should make the most of it. Perhaps the best way to look at the participation process is as a five-position continuum."

The Five-Position Participation Continuum

"Position 1 of the continuum represents *full participation by the manager,* who makes the decision without any direct input from his associates. He or she might order a report or analyze the raw data himself. In Position 2, the manager gets *minimal input*. For instance, in cases where I'm unhappy or unsure about a decision, I gather a few of my colleagues to talk it over. Then if I feel okay about it, I go with it. If I feel less than okay, I scratch it."

"And Position 3?"

"Position 3 is the halfway point where the manager may have made only a tentative decision or none at all. Therefore, he or she *invites ideas, suggestions and criticism* or solicits alternative decisions. But the manager remains responsible for the ultimate decision."

"And Position 4?"

"This is one step beyond Position 3. Here the manager *delegates most of the decision-making power to the group* provided the group has knowledge and experience with the particular output required."

"Then Position 5 must be complete control by the group?"

"Almost. The manager in this case *delegates everything to the group except accountability.* He or she asks for the output and allows the group to produce it."

Participation Continuum

Position 1: Full participation by manager.
Position 2: Minimal input from associates.
Position 3: Manager invites input but makes ultimate decision.
Position 4: Manager delegates most decision-making power to associates.
Position 5: Manager delegates all decision-making power to associates but retains accountability.

"How do you decide which position to take in a specific situation?"

"Each position has its advantages and disadvantages. Position 1, which is zero participation, works best for simple, routine decisions such as the color of my office walls or emergencies such as a fire. Position 5, where the group decides, is useful when I have neither the time nor the input to make a decision. However, this requires a good facilitator because leaderless groups can become paralyzed by indecision. I use Position 3 most often when I've arrived at a tentative decision. Then I call the group together and solicit criticisms, suggestions and alternatives.

"Or sometimes, Bill, I know I *need* a decision, but I haven't arrived at even a tentative one. I know I need more input, so I call a group together, tell them what's required and let them go to work. I participate as a facilitator and veto the final product only when I have a strong objection. Whatever the position, it is most important to create an atmosphere of free and open discussion."

"How do you do that, Ted?"

"It depends on whether the group is *generating* or *evaluating* ideas. If the group is generating ideas and alternatives, we place a ban on criticism and judgment, and we encourage all points of view. Nothing is too dumb to be put on the table. When the group is evaluating ideas and alternatives, criticism should be free and open. Then I play the devil's advocate and encourage everyone to criticize and evaluate everything."

"If I want a free and open discussion in my plant, how do I go about it?"

"Get yourself a good facilitator to motivate everyone to be as creative and open as possible and to be sensitive to all members of the group. Many people don't speak up for fear of sounding stupid. Others have a neurotic need to put down everyone else's ideas. Some people want to find out what positions the boss favors before committing themselves. Facilitating is not an easy job. The facilitator has to encourage, cajole, prod and push people to open up."

Facilitate To Generate Consensus and Support

"Isn't getting consensus and support from your associates the end result of this facilitation process?"

"Yes, but consensus is not the same as support. A consensus exists when everyone agrees. It implies support, but support can exist without consensus. People can support a decision with which they don't agree. Although consensus is desirable, sometimes it's not practical or possible or even necessary. Support, though, is *always* necessary. You can't get commitment without support. And support is much easier to achieve when everyone gets a chance to participate and voice possible objections."

"How do you know when you have consensus or support?"

"I don't assume I've got either until I confirm it. I play the devil's advocate again and knock down the decision, answer or idea a few times to see how well it can stand on its own. If I suspect the agreement is superficial, I press for further discussion. Premature consensus can be a symptom of earlier problems. Passive people may have suppressed their objections, or aggressive members may have railroaded their viewpoint through the group. When in doubt about the output, I go back to square one because I'm looking for *quality* output, not just *any* output."

"When you have agreed on output, Ted, what is next?"

"Write it down clearly and precisely. *Be specific* about who, what, where, when, how, how many. The statement 'We have decided to open a new store somewhere in the eastern region within the next year or so' defies implementation. But if you say 'We have decided to open a new 15-employee store on State Street in Boston by March of 1993, your plans are defined clearly and specifically."

"I can see that facilitating groups to get something accomplished isn't always easy."

"No, it isn't. And sometimes managers underestimate the skill involved, get frustrated and give up."

"How do *you* avoid that?"

"As a facilitator, I've learned to pay attention to two distinct levels in a group: (1) the *content* and (2) the *context*. The content is *what* the group is trying to accomplish—a decision, a solution to a problem, an idea or just an exchange of information. The context is *how* the group is accomplishing its task—the way people are interacting, whether discussion is flowing freely and whether people are nonjudgmental."

"Would you say that content is on the surface and context is beneath the surface?"

"Well put, Bill. A good facilitator needs dual perception. One minute you are deeply immersed in a problem; the next minute you realize the group process isn't working right. For example, Tracey hasn't said anything, Kevin is criticizing for no reason or Linda is interrupting too much."

"So what do you do?"

"I drop the content and deal with context. In dealing with content, I define the problem, clarify facts, request information, summarize viewpoints and critique ideas. When I turn to focusing on context, I discourage polarizing arguments, deal with personality conflicts, maintain open communication, press for a decision and check for consensus."

"But you must run into some obstacles. I know I would."

"We all do, Bill. The most frequent obstacles are *stalemates, personal conflicts* and *lack of participation skills.*

"For example, a group is moving right along and then it grinds to a halt before producing any output. Tough decisions aren't made because nobody wants to take the risk. There's your stalemate! A common cause is polarized discussion. By habit we get locked into black and white positions. We lay our egos on the line and refuse to budge. In these instances, there is no compromise and no consensus."

Facilitator's Obstacles

1. Stalemates
2. Personal conflicts
3. Lack of participation skills

"How do you go about breaking a stalemate, Ted?"

"One way is to press for more alternatives. Most arguments have more than two sides. Another way is to make a decision without consensus: the buck has to stop with the leader. And finally, you can press for a vote, but beware if the vote is not unanimous. You won't get consensus, and you'll still need support from the minority."

"What about the second obstacle, personal conflicts?"

"They can wreck participation. And they come from many sources—difficult people, hierarchies or power games—but you can minimize these conflicts."

"How?"

"First, try to recognize them *right away.* Listen carefully and observe. Second, try to separate the people from the problem by focusing on the personal problem directly or by skirting it and focusing attention on the matter at hand—the *group's task.* Of course, the best direction depends on the group's maturity and level of trust. Where there's a high level of trust, group members can deal with personal conflicts and won't feel they're being attacked. If you raise a personal issue, it's usually because it's seriously getting in the group's way. It usually works, however, to raise it in a nonthreatening way."

"The third obstacle was lack of participation."

"Sometimes we forget that some people just don't know *how* to participate well. They may be less articulate than their more verbal colleagues or they simply haven't had much experience talking in a group setting. Nevertheless, they may have a lot to contribute."

"How do you bring them out?"

"First you recognize that an obstacle exists and then you offer opportunities to build group skills. We have engaged consultants to teach group skills such as active listening. If your company is committed to training, teaching group skills can be a logical component of your overall training program. Workers today need far more than technical skills to succeed. Thus, if you want everyone in your company to become a self-manager, give them the opportunity to learn how."

"How would you summarize what makes participation work in your company?"

"I think the four important ingredients, Bill, are (1) a strong belief that participation *can* work, (2) respect for everyone in the group, (3) commitment and (4) patience."

"I can see that team building takes a lot of hard work."

"It does. Many managers opt to *restrict* participation. They make all the decisions themselves."

"Does that build mistrust?"

"Yes. When you discourage participation, you build mistrust by lowering—or even totally destroying—self-worth. Going it alone creates a weak business team, but participation encourages a strong, healthy, productive one."

"Time for me to be getting back to the plant," said Bill. "What about next week?"

"How about moving along one step further, Bill—from participation to creativity?"

"Sounds good to me. See you Wednesday!"

10

Creativity and Innovation

The restaurant was busy.

While Bill and I waited for a table, he said, "You promised we'd talk about *creativity* today, Ted. Does that sort of thing have any place in the practical world of business?"

"Indeed it does. Haven't you heard it said that the best way to predict the future is to invent it and keep on inventing it?"

"Yes, I have."

"Well, that takes creativity and innovation. The stiffer the competition gets, the more important innovation becomes. I know because my own business depends on constant innovation. Without it we'd all be out on the street in six months!"

We followed the waiter to our favorite table.

"I suppose you mean that creativity builds trust?"

I smiled. "You've got it, Bill! And do you know why?"

"No."

"Because the big stumbling block to creativity is fear—fear of being attacked, of sounding dumb or of being punished if your creative efforts turn out badly. Some companies view creativity as a threat to their status quo. But if you reduce fear and encourage self-expression, you can stimulate creativity and build trust."

"Isn't creativity something that a few lucky people, such as you, are born with?"

"Thanks for the compliment, Bill. But to answer your question, I'm deeply convinced as a result of my company's experience (and from what I've observed in other successful organizations) that creativity is *not* confined to a few born geniuses, that it *can* be learned."

Creativity Is Putting Old Ideas Together in New Ways

"Creativity is not pulling new ideas out of thin air—like a rabbit out of a hat. Rather, it's the ability to discover new relationships between *existing* things. It involves looking at them from a *new perspective,* putting old ideas together in *new ways* and rearranging old patterns into new patterns."

"Like a good cook combines well-known foods, spices and herbs in a different way and comes up with a delicious new dish?"

"That's a good metaphor, Bill. Creative people, in business *or* the kitchen, use not only knowledge and logic but also imagination and intuition."

"I've heard recently that one side of the brain is creative and the other is analytical, or something like that."

"I'm glad you brought that up, Bill, because I was just about to mention the split-brain theory."

"What's that?"

"Our brain has a left and a right hemisphere. The left brain is analytical and verbal, and the right brain is intuitive and visual. We use our left brain for speaking, writing, reading and analyzing. It abstracts, categorizes, judges and counts, and its tools are logic, reason and judgment."

"And the right brain?"

"We use our right brain to recognize patterns in complex data to help us understand analogies. The right brain visualizes and synthesizes. Its tools are intuition, insight and awareness."

"Can you give examples of each?"

"Yes. When you solve a problem by defining it, researching possible alternatives, assigning priorities and choosing alternatives, you are using your left brain. On the other hand, when you solve a problem by taking a walk, discussing it with colleagues, visualizing possible solutions or looking for similar problems, you are using your right brain."

"I suppose most people tend to lean one way or the other?"

"Probably, but few people are *completely* dominated by one side. The key to creativity is to use *both* sides. The creative person switches back and forth depending on the task."

"But in the business world, Ted, don't we stress logic, facts and figures—the left-brain functions?"

"Unfortunately, we do. We've been taught that this kind of thinking leads to effective problem solving. However, this ignores ambiguity and complexity and thereby limits thinking and inhibits creativity."

Four Steps To Encourage Creativity

"Are there specific steps you take to encourage creativity in your company, Ted?"

"Yes, there are four steps: (1) reinforce attitudes that promote creativity, (2) recognize that *everyone* is creative and can contribute, (3) provide the right environment and (4) recognize creativity when it happens."

Four Steps To Encourage Creativity

1. Reinforce attitudes that promote creativity.
2. Recognize that everyone is creative.
3. Provide the right environment for creativity.
4. Recognize creativity when it happens.

"How do you reinforce attitudes?"

"Creative people are optimistic, Bill. They *know* problems exist; they just have to uncover them. I encourage associates to focus on why things *can* be done, rather than on why they can't and to view problems as opportunities, not obstacles. You really have to believe that creativity is possible and then convince your associates of it. Once the creative process is in motion, it builds. If you encourage and reinforce it every day and in every way, it becomes part of your life-style."

"What about the second step, recognize that everyone can contribute?"

"I truly believe every person has something valuable to contribute. How often have you heard workers complain that they have ideas but nobody ever listens? If we take time to listen and *ask for* ideas and suggestions, we get good ones with very positive results. That brings us to the third step, provide the right environment for creativity. Have you ever heard the word *skunkworks,* Bill?"

"No, what does it mean?"

"It's an innovative technique that's becoming popular with many companies. A skunkworks is a place set apart from the regular plant or offices where creative people get together to work on special projects, where they can escape the constraints of the organizational bureaucracy, sidestep rules and throw cumbersome procedures out the window. All that counts are results."

"Sounds like a good idea."

"It is. Some companies set up a skunkworks not just because bureaucracy gets in the way of creativity, but because they're experimenting with a new product and get faster, better results working outside the normal organization. IBM did this in Florida to invent its personal computer."

"Isn't there a danger that you could set up a creative elite?"

"It's a risk, Bill. That's why our goal is to make the *whole company* a skunkworks where new ideas flourish in all departments."

"I believe your fourth step was recognize creativity when it happens?"

"Yes. In our meetings we're always looking for marketing ideas, book titles and ad slogans, so we're open to suggestions and ideas from every source. And when we get good ones—as we usually do—we recognize them. We find that recognizing people as innovators has a ripple effect. It encourages others to contribute suggestions and ideas."

"For example?"

"A while back we needed a catchy title for a book that eventually became one of our best-sellers. We solicited titles from our marketing people, editorial staff and writers. The title we eventually chose came from an accounting clerk. Recognizing her creativity had a very positive effect on everyone."

"And you do this in all areas of your company, Ted?"

"Yes. At our annual meeting we say, 'Ladies and gentlemen, we're doing a lot of things right, and some things we know we're doing wrong. What are some of the ways *you* think we can improve the company, our productivity and our profits?' We throw in questions such as 'What other products should we consider publishing or bringing to market?' 'What should we be doing that we're not doing?' 'What mistakes are we making, and what can we do about them?' 'How can each department improve its productivity?' We expect everyone to contribute and to listen to everyone else's ideas."

Four Steps to Creative Problem Solving

"I think you are saying that you can apply creativity to problem solving."

"That's right."

"How?"

"There are four steps involved in creative problem solving: (1) define the problem, (2) find the cause, (3) identify solutions and (4) integrate the solution."

"Isn't defining the problem pretty simple?"

"Not always, Bill. In my experience it's always tougher than it seems at first glance. And the way we define a problem determines the solutions we come up with. It means focusing *precisely* on critical issues and gathering as much information on them as possible. It's tempting, but unwise, to take a shortcut in this process."

Four Steps to Creative Problem Solving

1. Define the problem.
2. Find the cause.
3. Identify solutions.
4. Integrate the solution.

"Could you explain, Ted?"

"First let's define what a problem is—and what it isn't. Ask your colleagues what their problems are, and you'll hear complaints such as 'My people just aren't motivated,' 'Morale is going down the tubes along with productivity' or 'Quality control just can't do the job.' *But these aren't problems."*

"What are they?"

"They are symptoms, indications that something is wrong, but we have to probe deeper to find and define the real problem. We need to define a problem in the context of our production model. In this context, a problem is the gap between the output we want and the output we actually get. If we want ten proposals written and get only six, our problem is that we are minus four proposals."

"So low morale, for instance, wouldn't be a problem; it would be a symptom that something is wrong?"

"Right. We have to be careful not to confuse symptoms with problems and to remember that problems are effects, not causes. When the manager complains that his or her people just aren't motivated, he or she is talking about a cause, not a problem. The cause, low motivation, contributes to the problem: an output gap."

"Another confusion arises when *preferences* are mistaken for problems as in the statement 'Quality control just can't do the job.' In this case, quality control is not a problem. It's also not a symptom nor a cause. It's a preference. The manager isn't sure why quality control is not good enough. No measurement has been made. He or she just thinks it's below par."

"So we have to distinguish problems from causes, symptoms and preferences *before* we come up with solutions?"

"Right. We need to define actual output, desired output and the nature of the gap between them."

"How do we do that?"

"By asking *who, what, where, when* and *how* questions. For example: *Who's* involved in the situation? *What* exactly is going on? *Where* and *when* is it happening? *How* is it happening?"

"The more specifically you define your problem, the easier it is to solve it?"

"Yes. And one final question is this: even though there *is* a valid problem, *should* it be solved? Not every problem requires a solution. Sometimes the cost of solving a problem is just not worth the benefits to be gained."

"You mentioned that the second and third steps in creative problem solving are to find the causes and identify solutions."

"Yes, and if you have thoroughly *defined* your problem, you have probably identified some possible causes."

"So this is a left-brain skill?"

"Partly left and partly right. Many problems have multiple causes. Unless you brainstorm fully, you won't be able to identify them all. That's why I encourage my associates to think of as many causes as possible."

"How do you generate causes, solutions and ideas?"

"Brainstorming is the most common technique. But let me point out that the easiest way to destroy this process is to judge and criticize too early. In our groups we share this ground rule: generate first, criticize later."

"In other words, you suspend judgment."

"We avoid any kind of judgment, good or bad. We never say an idea is stupid, but we also guard against saying an idea is great. Instead, we try to generate as many alternatives as possible. Labeling ideas negatively stifles creativity. Labeling them positively limits ideas to whatever the group thinks is good."

"You encourage freewheeling, so to speak?"

"Exactly. Everyone should feel free to say outrageous things, to sound dumb, to loosen up. After all, the purpose of generating a number of causes, solutions and orders is not to find *the* right one. The purpose is to find as many right ones as possible. We welcome participants from different departments, too, because this simulates cross-fertilization of ideas. People from different backgrounds put new perspectives on problems."

"If we held a brainstorming session like that at my plant, what questions could I ask to stimulate cross-fertilization?"

"Well, you might ask any of the following questions: 'Assuming everything we know is wrong, what shall we do?' 'What can we do to make our problem as bad as possible?' or 'Imagine you're a completely naive customer. What do you see?'"

"What else can I do to encourage my associates to generate solutions to problems?"

"Urge them to welcome complexity, contradictions and ambiguity, not to ignore them. The real world is very complicated. Uncreative people are afraid of complexity and try to achieve order at all costs. They like simplistic, black-and-white solutions. Complexity is actually a springboard to sophisticated answers."

"So what do you do after you have generated a number of alternatives?"

"We then switch back to the left brain. We evaluate, criticize and judge. It's now time to play the devil's advocate and put each alternative under the microscope. Is idea X really practical? Why can't alternative Y be quantified? Will suggestion X really contribute to narrowing the output gap? The best way to evaluate alternatives is to compare them to criteria."

"How do you do that?"

"Your output goal helps you identify your criteria. Let's say you want to reduce defects in one of your products. Here are some criteria: reduce defects from 10 percent to 2 percent; reduce them by July 15; retain the same number of inspectors; keep additional expenses under a 5 percent increase; and maintain existing production volume."

"So you evaluate each alternative by referring to these criteria?"

"Yes. Focusing on the output you want and the gap that exists really helps discipline the process."

"Does this always work?"

"Usually, yet sometimes intuition tells you to go with an alternative that seems irrational but feels right. And some decisions are just too difficult to make if you use only logic. There are too many factors to keep straight, or there's something important involved that can't be measured. Your gut feeling may be a sense of the missing ingredient logic can't quite grasp."

"But what if your gut feeling really reflects bias or prejudice?"

"That's why I'm not advising you to throw out marketing surveys, statistics or logic. You can't run a business on whims. I'm just suggesting you add intuition to reason."

"And what about the fourth step to creative problem solving, integrate the solution?"

"Seeing the solution as a whole is the final stage. It means synthesizing and looking at the big picture. Integrating is a right-brain skill. It involves putting all the pieces of the puzzle together after you have taken them apart. Now you have a different picture. An integrative organization is one where communication is free and open. Everyone is encouraged to talk openly and exchange ideas."

"The goal is to bring as many good minds to bear on a problem as you can?"

"Right. Thinkers and doers are brought together, and both sides benefit. Ideas shown to be impractical are refined or tossed out. Operating problems are infused with new ideas. Both sides work to sort out the possible, the practical and the probable. Put another way, an *integrative company* is like a spider's web. The web is spun from strands of communication. When you develop this kind of quality network, you truly unlock the creative potential of your associates."

"But isn't there a danger of getting too creative, too carried away and maybe making some serious mistakes in the process?"

"Of course, but creative people aren't afraid to make mistakes. They know it's an important way to learn—and sometimes it's the only way. They view mistakes not as failures but as stepping-stones to success."

"But isn't it possible to make some bad mistakes that could be disastrous to the company?"

"Definitely. Therefore, it's important to clarify *acceptable* mistakes. All mistakes are acceptable except those that misuse company funds or damage the company's reputation. The two major questions are: (1) Can we afford a mistake? and (2) If a mistake is made, will it reflect badly on the company's image and reputation? The late William Gore of W. L. Gore & Associates used a good analogy. He said, 'Our enterprise is like a ship we're all in together. Boring holes above the waterline is not serious, but below the waterline, holes could sink our ship.'"

"I like your concept of creativity, Ted, and I'd like to try to put it into practice in my plant. I think we could benefit greatly."

"Go for it, Bill!"

"Any last words of advice on the subject, Ted?"

"I have just a few suggestions. Remember that creativity is *action*—not waiting around for the muse. Experiment, innovate and encourage your associates to do the same. Don't just *think up ideas; put them into practice.* The more you do that, the more you will learn from your experiences and the more creative you become."

"That sounds logical."

"Finally, don't forget to *reward creativity.* To *get* ideas isn't too difficult; to *keep on getting them* is what counts. Reward the good ideas and you will ensure a continuing supply."

"Thanks, Ted, I'll remember."

11

Time—How To Make It Work for You

Bill greeted me with a gentle admonishment.

"You didn't tell me last week what we'd talk about today."

I smiled. "Maybe it's time to talk about *time* and how we manage it to our advantage."

"Good! This must be another way you build trust, although I'm not sure how."

Time Management Is Self-Management

"Effective time management is a trust builder because it's really *self-management.* When you and your associates use your time wisely, it means you're managing *yourselves* responsibly. The results can make a big change for the better in all facets of your life."

"I know I don't manage my time effectively, Ted. I guess I'm a walking example of the old saying 'the hurrier I go, the behinder I get.' There just don't seem to be enough hours in a day to do all I need to do."

"Well, Bill, we all have just 24 hours a day. Getting *more* done doesn't require *more hours.* It demands *better management* of those 24 hours."

"I guess you're right, Ted."

"Do you know what would happen if you had 36 hours instead of 24 in your day, Bill?"

"No. What?"

"Parkinson's famous law would take over. Are you familiar with it?"

"I sure am, Ted. 'Work expands to fill the time available.'"

"Right. And with no significant difference in quality. Time and again, I've gotten the same—and sometimes better—results from a task completed in a few hours than from a similar one completed in a few days."

"But don't some jobs require our taking longer, if we do them well?"

"Yes. Some quality results require committing adequate time, such as special research or crafting a fine piece of furniture. However, there's an optimum interval beyond which time is wasted."

"But you seem to get so much accomplished and still have time for leisure activities like tennis, swimming and travel. How do you do it?"

"First, I make it a point to spend the *right amount of time* on the *right tasks*—those that contribute to quality productivity. There's another law—the Pareto Rule—that says 20 percent of our activities produce 80 percent of our accomplishments. It's important for me to identify the 20 percent of my activities that produce 80 percent of my results. I make certain these *always* get done. The time I spend carefully identifying and re-identifying these priority activities is well worth it! It keeps me on track."

"And what's your second secret for making the most of your time?"

"It's no secret, Bill. It's *planning*. Time management requires careful planning, advance planning, practical input/output planning."

"But my printing plant is a hectic place. There are crises all the time—deadlines, fires to be put out and always the *unexpected*. How can I plan around all that?"

"I once asked myself the same question, Bill. In my business, believe it or not, we have those same fires, crises and deadlines.

But I found out long ago that although we can't plan for every crisis—and must build some flexibility—we *can* plan for all the important things we need to get done. If we don't, none of them will get done, except occasionally by happy accident. To put it another way, if you can't control your time, other people's time will control you. And if you can't manage time well, you really can't manage anything else well."

"You feel that your managers—your associates—manage their time well?"

"Yes, I do. It's important to recognize and respect each other's ability to do this. That's just one more component of trust building."

Eight Steps to Effective Time Management

"So tell me, how do you go about time management planning? I suspect there are some specific steps you take."

"I do. There are eight steps, each equally important if you want to seize control of your life—business or personal.

"It sounds like good advice. Can you explain the steps one by one, Ted?"

"First, Step 1 is *find out how you are spending your time.* Record everything you do and how long it takes, even coffee breaks, traveling and personal phone calls. To be useful, the log needs to be detailed. Instead of simply entering 'writing a report' in your log, break the task into segments such as 'met with marketing people to talk about report,' 'studied research notes for report,' 'wrote first draft of report' and 'reviewed editorial comments.'"

"Why is all this detail so important?"

"Because you won't know which tasks to eliminate or delegate unless you know what they are and how much time they take."

"Isn't keeping a detailed log very time-consuming, Ted?"

"Not if you avoid extremes. You don't need to go into minute detail about every coffee break, but do put in all the essentials. Keeping this log will be a real eye-opener."

Eight Steps to Controlling Your Life

1. Find out how you are spending your time.
2. List your goals in order of priority.
3. Compare what you are doing with what you should be doing.
4. Set aside time to plan and write a "to do" list.
5. Break complicated tasks into manageable pieces.
6. Identify tasks that can be delegated, postponed or eliminated.
7. Block out and schedule your day.
8. As the day progresses, review and update your list."

"How?"

"Because what you *think* you are doing and what you are actually doing will probably be pretty far apart."

"For instance?"

"You may find you spend literally hours each day on totally unimportant tasks and leave the important ones untouched. Interruptions and excessive paperwork eat up your days. You'll probably also find that you are doing some things simply because you enjoy doing them, not because they need doing."

"Even without keeping a log, I'd have to plead guilty, Ted. But I see the value in keeping one. Now what about Step 2, *list your goals in order of priority?"*

"Setting goals and priorities is an important time-management technique. If you have followed the process we outlined several weeks ago, you have already identified your output and the tasks necessary to produce that output. These tasks become your short-term goals."

"What happens after I've listed them?"

"Then you're ready for Step 3: *Compare what you are doing with what you should be doing.* In other words, place your output goals next to the entries in your time log and see how they correlate."

"For example?"

"Let's say one of your goals is to improve productivity by talking with employees. Another goal is to listen to your employees' problems by meeting with them informally. But your time log tells you that you have spent only two hours doing both in the past two weeks. Is an average of one hour per week sufficient to fulfill these goals? If not, you have some changes to make. As you do your time analysis, you'll undoubtedly find plenty of time wasters—irrelevant phone calls, unnecessary interruptions, etc. But keep at it! Go through your log, compare each activity with your goals and in each case ask yourself this question: 'Can I cut the time I devote to this task or delay it—or eliminate it altogether?"

"And what's Step 4?"

"*Set aside time to plan and write a to do list.* You can do this either at the beginning or end of the day. I prefer late afternoon. The day's activities are still fresh in my mind, and I can adjust the next day's schedule according to what was—or was not—accomplished. If you're a morning person, set aside 15 to 20 minutes before the day begins—before the world arrives with its problems at nine o'clock."

"How do I go about drawing up this list?"

"List everything you have do in a given day—people to talk with, meetings to attend, projects to finish, etc. I use a piece of paper with three columns labeled A, B and C in that order of priority. This way I can record and prioritize simultaneously. But any system that works for you is okay."

"As long as I put in writing?"

"Yes. *Planning must be in writing.* You can't keep it all in your head."

"What about long-term projects or future conferences?"

"For these, I use a weekly/monthly/yearly planning guide. I write down all known deadlines and scheduled events. Then I work backward and block out the estimated time to complete the tasks. Just don't let your system get too complicated. Keep it simple!"

"How?"

"That brings us to Step 5. *Break complicated tasks into manageable pieces.* Accomplishing these easy-to-complete subtasks builds confidence."

"Can you illustrate, Ted?"

"Yes. Let's say the tasks is to write a report. We'll divide this into five subtasks: collect computer data, review seven previous reports, talk to division managers to get input, order financial stats from accounting and develop rough subject outline. Now estimate how long each subtask will take and block out the appropriate time. Your estimates may not be exact, but they will improve with practice."

"It seems as though this might be a good way to avoid procrastination. I find it's tempting to do the small, trivial things that I can finish quickly and ignore the biggies that are breathing down my neck."

"You're so right, Bill. And subdividing big jobs offers more opportunity for positive reinforcement. You can reward yourself or your associates every time a subtask is completed. This brings us to Step 6: *Identify tasks that can be delegated, postponed or eliminated.*"

"Delegating and eliminating shouldn't be too difficult."

"Sometimes this is easier said than done, Bill. Perhaps you are doing a favor for someone. Or you may actually like picking up other people's slack. Or you simply *enjoy* doing a particular job. Or you are doing the job because you've *always* done it."

"But these don't all sound like bad reasons, Ted."

"They're not, and even if it's not the best use of your time, you may want to continue doing something you really enjoy. Fine! The purpose of time-management isn't to turn you into a robot. It's to make you aware of what you are doing and to help you evaluate the costs and benefits of your activities."

"What about postponing tasks? Couldn't that be an excuse for procrastinating?"

"I like to think of postponement, Bill, as *intelligent procrastination.* Your deadlines can tell you what to postpone if you know how long an activity takes. Decide *when* you can start a task that need not be started now. That will free up your time for more urgent tasks."

"Well, now we're at Step 7, *blocking out and scheduling your day.* How does this differ from writing the 'to do' list in Step 4?"

"In the 'to do' list, you listed your day's projects in priority order. In Step 7, you're actually scheduling them within the time constraints you have available."

"I guess it's Parkinson's Law again, Ted! If you don't block out tasks, one or two of them could balloon into situations that fill your whole day—or week."

"That's a real danger. I recommend scheduling A-priority tasks first to make sure they get done. Some managers disagree and prefer warming up with simple C-priority jobs such as making easy phone calls or doing routine paperwork. They claim this gets them psyched for A activities later."

"That's what I do, Ted. I *think* I'll clear up my desk of trivia before I settle down to serious business, which I frequently never get to!"

"I used to do that, too, and with the same negative results. But I learned! Of course, it's a good idea to schedule high-priority jobs when your mental energy is at its highest level, and if that happens to be in the afternoon, you may be justified in postponing A-priority jobs until then. For me, morning is best, so that's when I tackle tasks that require intense concentration."

"Then you do B and C activities later in the day?"

"Right. Routine correspondence and simple administrative matters come later in the afternoon. I also batch similar C tasks *together.* This saves time 'shifting gears.'"

"Do you ever leave a little time *unscheduled,* Ted?"

"Good point, Bill. I set aside an hour or two of free time each day if I can. This gives me some slack for the unexpected, and for occasional breaks and periods of rest."

"Doesn't your planning *ever* go awry, Ted? Get knocked into a cocked hat by some sudden emergency?"

I smiled. "Sure, Bill. Nobody's perfect, but this brings us to Step 8: *As the day progresses, review and update your list.* Some jobs take more or less time than expected. Fires sometimes have to be put out, so it's important to temper discipline with flexibility.

That's why I do my planning with a pencil; it's easier to make changes."

"And I suppose you carry your list with you everywhere?"

"I do. I use a small notebook and keep it at my fingertips for easy reference and to record commitments as soon as I make them. It's a good motivator, too."

"How is that?"

"Let's say I'm having a conversation with an associate and a problem arises requiring action, such as a future meeting. I agree to it on the spot and pencil it immediately into my planning guide. That way I don't have to go into the old delaying routine by telling the associate that I have to go back to my office, check my calendar and get back to him or her. I can do it right then and there. It saves time and sends a positive message to my associates."

"I've learned a lot today, Ted, and I'm anxious to put it all into practice. But there are several areas you've mentioned where I always seem to run into problems."

"Name some."

"Well, I think my most vulnerable spot is dealing with interruptions. They're so annoying, yet so difficult to eliminate."

Control Interruptions

"Most of us tolerate too many interruptions, Bill. We hate to be rude and want to be helpful. It's flattering to see yourself as someone else's problem solver. But if you're going to make your schedule work, you've got to stop and think before you respond to unscheduled requests. Ask yourself questions such as 'Is what I'm being asked to do more important than what I had planned to do in that time slot? Could someone else do it better? Is it important at all?' If your answers are 'no,' then don't be squeamish. Say no to the request; most people will understand. Another good way to deal with interruptions is to *prevent* them. I let my associates know when I don't want to be disturbed. I close my door and ask my secretary to hold my calls."

"Is *how* you say no important, too?"

"Very. If you're not accustomed to saying no, you may come off as abrupt or even hostile. If you are *afraid* to say no, you may sound wishy-washy. I use the following six guidelines for saying no:

1. I say no firmly without equivocating, and I don't add 'I'm sorry.'
2. I follow up with an explanation of *what* I'm saying no to and why I'm saying it, as in 'I'm not willing to do that because . . .' or 'I'm uncomfortable doing that because . . . .'
3. If I can say no now but yes later, I do. If I know *when* I can say yes, I tell the person and if not, I ask for time to plan.
4. I soften the blow by acknowledging the importance of the request before saying no, as in 'I understand it's important for you to get some help on this right now, but I can't do it now because . . . .'
5. I say yes to *part of the request* if I can but no to the part I can't or don't want to do.
6. If the person won't take no for an answer, I *persist* and keep on saying no as politely as possible because I find most people eventually get the message."

"What if the person doesn't get the message or becomes hostile?"

"He or she is trying to force me to say yes. I acknowledge this kind of hostility by reflecting it back. I just say no again. Saying no can be difficult, especially if you think you'll lose respect and approval. But you won't. When people know your limits, they respect them."

"It sounds like good advice to me, Ted."

"Do you have any more problems, Bill?"

"There's one final one—how to stop drowning in paper. I think paperwork is my worst time waster!"

Cut Down on Paperwork

"We do sometimes seem to be sinking in a sea of memos, forms, reports and computer printouts. Why? Because it's easy to produce paper and even easier to copy it. But let's remember, Bill, *paper is not output,* except in publishing companies, consulting firms or government agencies. When I order a report from one of my departments, it's not output for me, but it is for the person assigned to write it. I encourage my associates not to *transmit* paperwork but rather to *add value to it.* If they don't, they're just passing the buck. They're simply reporting."

"How do you add value to raw data?"

"Some examples might be a report that summarizes the results of a meeting, a computer printout that answers specific questions or excerpts from a conversation keyed to specific issues."

"You said that we're drowning in paperwork because it's easy to produce and copy it. But there must be some reason that runs deeper."

"There is, Bill. Mistrust. And mistrust leads to CYA—Cover Your Ass. Everything put in writing can serve as potential evidence if needed later. Should a conflict arise, everything is on the record. I submit that the level of mistrust in a company is in direct proportion to the size of its files."

"Are there other reasons for all this paper?"

"Yes. Paper is used to keep people at a distance. Memos are written when conflicts are too uncomfortable to deal with personally, or reports are written to impress superiors. Sign-off sheets pin down accountability. Procedural forms and manuals are often merely efforts to control. Many managers unfortunately believe that written procedures will be followed and written rules obeyed."

"But they aren't?"

"No. Overcontrol usually backfires. Long, unreadable instructions are not read or understood. A list of 200 rules is simply ignored. So whenever my associates or I are faced with questionable paperwork, we ask questions such as: 'Is the proposed paper the output?' 'If not, what does it contribute to the output?' 'Does the paperwork add to complexity or simplify it?' 'Does this particular form have any purpose at all?' 'What would happen if the report were not written?' 'Will this paperwork accomplish anything better than a face-to-face conversation?' 'Does the proposed paperwork add value to data or information?' If we can't answer yes to these questions, we scrap the existing paperwork or decide not to produce more."

"Managing time effectively isn't easy, is it, Ted?"

"No, it's easier to continue old habits. But managing time wisely is managing *yourself* wisely. And time is all you've really got. Incidentally, in my company we fill out time analysis worksheets periodically—approximately every six months—to see how we're spending our time and what changes are in order. I've brought along a copy of the worksheet if you'd like to have it."

"Thanks, I would. And thanks, too, for a good one today, Ted. As always, you've given me a lot to think about—and to put into practice."

"See you next week, Bill. We'll talk about motivation."

(Sample)

Time Analysis Worksheet

Name: Josephine Curtis Department: Order Processing
Position: Customer Service Rep Reports to: John McElroy

Activity by Type	Time Spent	Percentage of Total Time
Reading & sorting mail	1/2 hour	6.25%
Researching customer inquiries and complaints	1 hour	12.5%
Composing & typing customer letters	4 hours	50%
Filing	1/4 hour	3.125%
Photocopying	1/4 hour	3.125%
Entering data into computer	1/2 hour	6.25%
Relief on switchboard	1 1/2 hours	18.75%

Time Wasters	Cause	Solution	When/To
Getting side-tracked by others when researching.	I allow distractions.	Firmly decline distractions.	7/1/92 12/31/92
Overtime on switchboard relief.	Switchboard operator late.	Discuss with her & with manager.	Immediately.
Noisy workplace.	Overcrowded.	Discuss expansion at dept. meeting.	Immediately.
Daydreaming.	In love.	Firmly postpone all thoughts to lunch hour.	Immediately.

Notes:
Putting this on paper is very helpful.

Signed (Employee) /Date Signed (Supervisor) /Date

Note: The following page contains a blank form that may be reproduced for your personal use if you wish. Or, you may want to modify it and create your own.

Time Analysis Worksheet

Name: ______________________ Department: ____________________

Position: ______________________ Reports to: ____________________

Activity by Type	Time Spent	Percentage of Total Time

Time Wasters	Cause	Solution	When/To

Notes:

____

____

______________________________ ______________________________

Signed (Employee) /Date Signed (Supervisor) /Date

12

Motivation

Bill was waiting for me with a broad smile.

"You seem to be in high spirits today," I commented as we made our way to our corner table.

"I am, Ted. Since you said we'd talk about *motivation,* I've been wondering how this translates into trust building. I'm sure it does!"

I smiled, too. "When I motivate, I focus on problems, not people. People are never problems; they're solutions. And if you consider them as solutions, you'll build trust."

Focus on Problems, Not People

We ordered the crab cioppino.

"Do you mean that if you consider people a problem, you'll build *mistrust?"*

"Definitely. So many managers make this mistake. They try to find *someone to blame.* This attitude degrades workers and robs them of their dignity and self-respect. That's why I concentrate on *output gaps* rather than personalities. This is because I know that if I attack my associates personally, their self-esteem will crumble, and they will become defensive and resentful. When associates think *they* are the problem, they will be reluctant to take any responsibility for solving the problem at hand."

"In other words, you concentrate on the deed, not the doer?"

"Right, but I make sure what I'm focusing on really needs doing."

"For example?"

"Well, let's say you notice your associates are overextending their coffee breaks. You could order *everyone* to limit their breaks to ten minutes, but this could cause them to feel like children getting their wrists slapped. Your associates will resent it, and the result might be the opposite of what you want—lower rather than higher productivity. Perhaps you're merely bothered by people who don't always *look busy* and there really is no output gap. Or perhaps the coffee klatch really *is* talking about work-related problems because they have no other opportunity to get together to discuss them. Maybe you need to give them another place to do this, such as the conference room. Above all, get all the facts before you act."

"But what if we do face a real problem, Ted?"

"Then find out what's causing it. Performance problems have three basic causes: (1) your associates are *incapable* of performing, (2) they are capable but *won't* perform or (3) they are capable and willing to perform, but *performance isn't possible.* Another way of putting it is to ask if your associates are *ready, able* and *willing* to perform."

Three Causes of Performance Problems

1. Associates are incapable of performing.
2. Associates are capable of performing, but they are unwilling.
3. Associates are capable and willing to perform, but performance is impossible.

"Please explain, Ted."

"If my associates are not ready to perform effectively, I know they lack skill, training or practice. I can't blame someone for a poor job if he or she doesn't know how to do a good one. The associate may never have learned the skills he or she needs for the job or may need to upgrade existing skills. Perhaps he or she is simply out of practice."

"Do you provide training for your employees?"

"Yes, indeed. As work becomes more dependent on mental labor, success becomes more dependent on constant learning. Managers need to know *they* are responsible for establishing a *climate of learning,* and we encourage everyone to take advantage of learning opportunities, seminars, books and courses. Training and education are *everyone's* responsibility. It's not up to the personnel department to train people. It's everyone's job, and the more experienced colleagues are often the best teachers."

"What if your associates are ready to perform successfully, but are unable to do so?"

"Then I look to see what obstacles are in the way. Associates may not have enough input. Or they may lack the *right kind of input.* This includes materials, equipment, space and time. They also may lack a properly designed job and a decent place to work. Input is anything a person needs to do a good job."

"And it's up to the manager to provide the input?"

"Yes, if he or she is a good manager. And the manager must look at his or her own performance, too. Is he or she giving proper directions, delegating properly and providing effective feedback? All of this goes back to *trust.* If you trust your associates, you'll take a careful look at their work environment before you lay the blame on them."

"You mentioned *willingness* on the part of your associates as the third ingredient of good performance. Would you elaborate, Ted?"

"Yes. Even when an associate is ready and able to perform, he or she may lack willingness—or motivation. I find this out by asking myself this question: If the associate's life depended on it, could he or she perform? If the answer is yes, then you have a motivation problem. For instance, if my life depended on it, I *could* run a mile in five minutes, but even if you put a gun to my head, I couldn't play a piano concert at Carnegie Hall. The concert requires a skill I don't have, so no amount of motivation would bring it off."

Motivation Is a Combination of Needs and Incentives

"So what do you do when you have a motivation problem among your associates?"

"There are two kinds of motivation—(1) *internal,* which includes a person's needs and desires and (2) *external,* which includes incentives. Our needs create drives that compel us to act, and the psychologists tell us we have five levels of need: (1) *physiological,* (2) *safety and security,* (3) *social,* (4) *status and recognition and* (5) *self-fulfillment.* Physiological need, of course, includes food, shelter, oxygen, exercise and rest. The need for safety and security means protection against danger, threats and deprivations of physiological needs. Social need is that deepfelt urge to be part of a meaningful group—the need for affiliation, friendship and love."

"And what about the need for status and recognition, Ted? Is this something a good manager provides?"

"It is, Bill. We all value our personal worth and dignity, and we need recognition and respect from other people. A good manager sees that we get this. He or she also helps associates meet their highest-level need for self-fulfillment—that is, realizing their full potential and becoming as competent and creative as they can."

"But *all* needs are important, aren't they?"

"They are. I like to think of needs as spokes on a wheel. Each spoke represents a level of need, and when all are met, the wheel rolls smoothly. In earlier times, managers assumed it was enough to meet their workers' basic needs. Workers were paid just enough to keep them and give them minimum job security. Today workers—rightfully—expect recognition and fulfillment. This brings us to the second kind of motivation I mentioned—external motivation, or *providing incentives.*"

"If you provide enough incentives, people will do a good job?"

"You must provide enough of the *right kind* of incentives, Bill. It's important to meet your associates' needs, but as psychologist Douglas MacGregor said, 'Satisfied needs are not motivators.' Only unsatisfied needs can motivate. That's why a job that's challenging provides incentive."

"Do too many managers fail to provide this?"

"Yes, and they just don't bother to find out what their employees' perceived needs are. A study was recently done wherein employees were asked to rate a list of job-satisfaction factors from one to ten (the most important to the least important), and managers were given the same list to guess what their employees would come up with."

"Were the results different?"

"Very. Employees placed appreciation of their work, feeling 'in' on things and understanding of personal problems at the top of the list, with money down in fifth place. Managers put wages and job security first, and appreciation of work was down in eighth place. In another study, managers listed money as the number-one incentive, while employees rated it fifth. Employees, on the other hand, rated interesting work first and recognition second."

"So what's the moral?"

"The moral is: Perceptions differ. To find out what my associates consider important, I don't *assume*, I *ask*."

"What are some of the incentives you provide, Ted?"

"Well, despite the fact that the poll I mentioned showed money down in fifth place with employees, I find that my associates rate it higher. So we use *salary increases* and *bonuses* as incentives. We find, however, that it is important to tie salary increases and bonuses to *specific performance*, not just to give annual raises. And another tangible reward we provide is what we call 'a piece of the action.'"

"You mean stock in the company?"

"Not exactly. I established a better solution that doesn't involve legal complexities such as SEC regulations or problems. Instead, we have what we call a unit share agreement. Some people call this phantom stock. Key employees are issued unit shares equivalent to ownership in the company as they earn them. As the company grows, the unit shares appreciate."

"What about *benefits* as an incentive, Ted?"

"Benefits usually come as part of the salary package, so we don't have as much latitude in varying benefits with performance. We do have another incentive, though, that our associates like very much. We call it *freedom,* meaning time off, fewer restrictions or no time clocks. It sends this powerful message of trust: if you can produce, we'll reward you with more freedom."

"Are there other incentives you use, Ted?"

"Yes. One such incentive I call *advancement/growth/challenge.* Successful performers want greater challenge, more responsibility and an opportunity for personal growth. This can mean a promotion, a lateral transfer or a challenging project."

"For instance?"

"Many skilled workers or engineers don't want promotion into a management position. Therefore, a number of companies have set up parallel career paths for them whereby top technical people get a chance to invent new products or develop new processes."

"One final incentive, which is perhaps the most potent reward of all, is *recognition.* Ways to recognize good performance are limited only by your imagination. They can include letters of commendation, public praise, citations, prizes or awards. But there are several caveats, Bill. *Formal* awards can create unnecessary competition, so nonwinners can feel like losers even though they shouldn't. My company has used both formal and informal awards, but our employee awards are voted by the employees themselves. Because they 'own' the awards, they don't see themselves as losers."

"What you've told me, Ted, confirms the saying 'different strokes for different folks.' Incentives differ with the individual, and I, as a manager, need to be sensitive to the needs and desires of my employees."

"So true, Bill. And you learn by asking and listening. We occasionally have goal-setting sessions where I ask questions such as: 'Where do you see yourself going in the company?' 'What makes work satisfying?' and 'What are some ways it can be more satisfying for you?' I've found that once people realize I care, they open up and reveal what really motivates them."

Identify Your Motivators

"I need to motivate my people more at the plant, Ted. Do you have any final suggestions on how to do this?"

"Yes. Remember first that *everyone* is motivated—unless they're dead. You just have to *identify* your motivators—and de-motivators."

"Which are?"

"First, using the stick (literally) is a *negative physical motivator*, but this is bodily abuse and is rarely used today, at least in our country. However, there still is a lot of *negative psychological demotivation* going on—that is, fear and threats, such as lowering wages, cutting benefits or worst of all, threatening to fire workers. Finally, there's the *positive psychological motivator*—the carrot—but I should emphasize that it must be the *right kind of carrot*."

"What is that?"

"I focus on behavior, not attitudes. *Attitudes* are feelings and emotions. *Behavior* is what people do and say. And *consequences* are what happens as a result of behavior."

"Can you give me an example, Ted?"

"Yes. Let's say your secretary, Nancy, comes to work angry—that's an attitude. She makes a number of mistakes in a report you've given her—that's a behavior. You read the report and give it back, telling her to stay late and do it right—that's the consequence. Nancy gets angrier but stays and rewrites the report. However, there are still a number of errors. You blame this on Nancy's poor attitude, yet you know you cannot change this directly. What you can change is what *you* do—the consequences. You can talk to her about her work methods. Ask her how they can be improved and together come to a better, clearer understanding of a satisfactory final product—a report without mistakes."

"Do you have any final words on incentives, Ted?"

"Remember that even positive incentives may not always work. Human beings have freedom of choice, an independent will. The best you can do is create an environment filled with the right kind of incentives, remembering that motivation is a *combination* of needs and incentives. A manager can understand needs; he or she can't manage them but can only manage incentives."

"How?"

"Let's leave that for next week, Bill!"

13

Rewards

"Are we going to talk about rewards today, Ted?"

"We'll talk about rewarding *results,* Bill. I have a saying that if you reward results, you'll get them."

Reward Results and You'll Get Them

"Is that another trust builder?"

"Right. By rewarding *output,* you build trust because you strengthen your associates' self-worth and ability. Showing your faith and confidence in them this way sends a powerful message of trust."

"You are really influencing behavior here, aren't you, Ted?"

"Yes, by influencing the consequences."

"What do you mean?"

"By consequences I mean things that happen that are associated with specific behavior. First I identify *positive* and *negative* consequences or stimuli. Behavioral scientists call positive stimuli *reinforcers.* Examples of reinforcers are a good meal, a sunny day, money, etc. Telling one of your associates that he or she is doing a good job is a reinforcer."

"And negative stimuli?"

"Negative stimuli are *aversive stimuli,* which are things we don't like or want to avoid, such as disapproval and unfair criticism. Telling one of your associates he or she is doing a bad job is an aversive stimulus. Of course, whether a stimulus is a reinforcer or aversive depends on your perspective."

"For example?"

"One of your associates turns in an excellent report. He or she deserves a significant reward, so you give the associate a much more responsible assignment because you see this as a reinforcer or reward for work well done. The associate may perceive it as such or may see it as an aversive stimulus or *punishment* for a job well done."

"So a smart manager needs to know and empathize with his associates?"

"Yes. And in this behavioral process, you need to ask these questions: Is desired behavior being punished? Is undesired behavior being reinforced? and Does behavior result in *any* consequences?"

"So your goal is to reinforce behavior that produces quality output and discourage behavior that doesn't?"

"Right. I find the first step in influencing tomorrow's behavior is to observe today's behavior carefully. Let's say you are concerned about an associate's motivation. Describing his or her behavior as 'low motivation' is pointless. Instead, you need to target the *specific* behavior, such as arriving late three times a week, turning in work late twice a month or refusing to sign up for available projects. Also pay close attention to the consequences—the *immediate* consequences. Your swift reaction is more important than what you say three weeks later."

Catch People Doing Something Right

"But what about specific behavior that shows high motivation and *increases* output?"

"I especially like to recognize that behavior. I call it *catching people doing something right.* We focus on desirable behavior and quickly reinforce it instead of looking for mistakes to punish."

"You mean you use the carrot rather than the stick?"

"Exactly. Praise is a powerful motivator—far more so than punishment. It makes you wonder why so many managers use praise so sparingly. You know, if you urged those managers to use praise more often, you'd probably hear statements such as 'Why? Our workers get paid for doing a good job, don't they?', 'I don't want to swell their heads!' and 'It's not up to me to make them feel good. My job is to be on the lookout for things that can go wrong!"

"Do you think that's because a lot of managers think of themselves as troubleshooters rather than reinforcers?"

"Unfortunately, they do. Of course, there's nothing wrong with discovering mistakes. The problem arises when managers stress punishment to the exclusion of reinforcement. This builds a negative work climate. It's what I call the 'half-full glass' versus the 'half-empty glass.'"

Use Effective Reinforcers

"Do you have any specific suggestions for effective reinforcement?"

Three Effective Reinforcers

1. Personalized reinforcers
2. Reinforcers that fit the performance
3. Immediate reinforcers

"I do. First, we find *personalized* reinforcers work best. Personalizing takes communication and observation. Not everyone reacts in the same way to the same stimuli. Personalizing also needs to be directed at a specific person for a specific behavior. Praising a group is all right on occasion, but it's not as effective as individual praise. One of our managers has established a procedure that works very well as a reinforcer. She reads aloud to the staff all letters received from clients praising individual staff members for their performance."

"And what are your other tips for effective reinforcing, Ted?"

"Reinforcers should *fit the performance*—that is, give small rewards for small successes and big rewards for big successes. In addition, effective reinforcement *should follow closely the desired behavior.* Immediate praise is more effective than putting a letter in a personnel file three weeks later. And letting people take Friday off after completing a big job is more effective than adding a day to everyone's summer vacation."

"You don't think reinforcement can get out of hand, Ted?"

"We once had an occasion where we thought maybe it was going in that direction, so we asked some of our associates who had been praised recently about this, and all of them gave us the same message: 'You can't praise too much. Keep on doing what you're doing!' Since then we have looked for reasons to praise and reward, whether it's lunch with the boss, a drink after work or a beer with the guys in the warehouse. The results have been very positive. The more praise there is, the more output."

"Does reinforcement *always* work, Ted?"

"Sometimes it doesn't. Let's say you have analyzed behavior and followed the principles we've talked about closely, yet nothing changes. You may be tempted to go back to the old routine of looking for mistakes and punishing people. *Don't!* Stick with it."

"What are some of the reasons reinforcement doesn't always bring results?"

Why Reinforcement May Not Work

1. It's conditional.
2. It's inappropriate.
3. There's too much peer pressure.

"It may not work if you make it *conditional.* You know the 'yes/but' response. We've all heard it. For example, the boss comes over to your desk and says, 'That was a great report, Al, but can't you cut down on some of the mistakes next time?' Managers who do this may think their praise is getting across, but it's not. Their victims learn quickly that praise is just a prelude to criticism."

"So positive reinforcement should always be unconditional?"

"Yes. And another reason reinforcement doesn't work is that managers quit too soon. Habits cultivated over a long period of time can't be unlearned overnight. You need to keep at it. It's important, too, that a reinforcer be *appropriate.* If *more* work is perceived as punishment, by all means avoid using it. And if you encourage free and open communication at your plant and spend a lot of time with your people, you'll learn what is—and is not—reinforcing to them."

"Are there any other reasons why reinforcement doesn't work, Ted?"

"The final reason is *peer pressure.* You may do a great job reinforcing an associate for punctuality only to find that her peer group looks with disdain on punctuality as too conformist—as 'uncool'—so your efforts are negated. Anyone who has taught in high school understands well the awesome power of peer pressure. It doesn't disappear when we grow up. If one of your departments reinforces mediocre performance while you're trying to reinforce excellence, you will be paddling upstream against a stiff current."

"What do you do if the behavior you want *never* happens? How can you reinforce something that never happens?"

"I never say 'never,' Bill. Rome wasn't built in a day, and behavior doesn't change overnight. One way to reinforce something that doesn't *seem* to be happening is by *shaping.*"

"What's that?"

"It's the process of reinforcing any small steps in the right direction. You and Marge are raising kids, so you know you don't get a baby to walk by rewarding him only when he's able to sprint across the living room. First you reward sitting, then crawling and finally, the first few steps. Similarly, if you want 64 percent of your widgets produced with zero defects, you won't reach that goal by reinforcing only that final goal. Instead, you reinforce successive improvements, or *small wins.* Look for singles, not just home runs."

"What about dealing with repeated undesirable behavior?"

"We simply extinguish it. Use the reverse process, which means *not following* bad behavior with a reinforcer. But you've got to be careful not to extinguish good behavior. In other words, if you've been repeatedly and consistently praising high performance and you suddenly stop praising it, you may extinguish the desirable behavior altogether. Then it will just stop happening. You have to keep kindling the flames, Bill, or your company fire may just go out."

We picked up our checks.

"It's been a good one, Ted. What's the topic for next week?"

"Since we talked about rewards today, how about punishment—positive, of course—next time?"

"I'll be waiting!"

14

Nobody's Perfect

As promised, Bill was waiting.

"Ted, I have some qualms about discussing punishment today. It sounds so ominous, so negative."

"Not really, Bill. This is the aversive stimuli we mentioned briefly last week. Some people call it constructive criticism, and they mean let's make punishment *useful.*"

"I suppose you're going to tell me that punishment's a trust builder."

"Believe it or not, I am. All of us need to know when we've done something *wrong,* as well as when we've done something *right.* We trust managers who let us know when we've gotten off the track."

"As long as they do it the right way?"

"Yes. Managers who use punishment wisely earn respect."

"Is there any scientific basis for this?"

"There is. Behavioral scientists define punishment as connecting a behavior with an aversive stimulus. An aversive stimulus can be anything that causes physical or emotional pain. Examples are the loss of some benefit or privilege, such as money, status or position, or disapproval in the form of criticism, reprimands, punishments or condemnations."

Negative Punishment Is Ineffective

"What else do your scientists tell us?"

"They say that punishment must be *effective*. Too many managers use *ineffective punishment* that only increases fear and mistrust with no positive change in behavior. This is *negative punishment* and is seen by the recipient as a *personal attack.*"

"And that lowers self-esteem?"

"Yes, and negative punishment has other negative effects."

"Such as?"

"Negative punishment can tell a person to *stop* doing something wrong, but it doesn't tell him or her how to *start* doing something right. It also creates mistrust. The victim begins to associate the punisher with the punishment. He or she thinks a punishment is imminent even when no punishment is forthcoming. Once a manager is associated with pain, it sticks. If he or she tries to discard the tough-guy image for a more humane one, it only confuses his or her subordinates, and they become even more suspicious and mistrustful."

"What are some of the other negative effects, Ted?"

"Negative punishment sometimes spreads its net *too* wide and suppresses desirable behaviors. For example, if you punish one of your managers for taking risks—say, a new marketing approach that doesn't happen to work out—then the manager is reluctant to take any risks again. He or she is afraid to try something new another time. Thus, negative punishment encourages conformity and rigid behavior."

"Also remember that punishment works *only when the punisher is present*. Some managers, like parents, think if they make the punishment severe enough, it will stick in their absence. Of course, it doesn't. It's the classic situation of while the cat's away, the mice will play."

"Is there anything else on the negative side, Ted?"

"There's just one more thing: *avoidance learning.*"

"What's that?"

"Let me give you an example. The manager asks, 'Dave, where's the report I asked for?' and Dave says, 'I'm sorry, I haven't finished it yet.' The manager replies, 'Why not? You had as long as anyone else.' Dave then responds, 'Not really. The research people just gave me the data.' Dave is excusing himself, but the manager gives in and says 'Well, maybe I should talk to the research people about that.' By *turning off* the punishment in response to Dave's excuse, the manager is teaching Dave how to avoid punishment. Avoidance learning comes wrapped in all sorts of packages: excuses, rationalizations, shifting blame, feigning helplessness, etc. It sugarcoats serious problems and encourages associates to become yes-men or yes-women. It also fosters manipulation, dishonesty and mistrust."

"Doesn't negative punishment also encourage *resistance,* as in fighting back?"

"I'm glad you mentioned that, Bill. It does, and even when workers don't openly fight back, they do it deviously through apathy, absenteeism or outright sabotage. But let's talk about *positive punishment.*"

"Good! I'm ready for that."

"Positive punishment can work *for* you, and its rewards include a decrease in fear, an increase in mutual trust and respect and the emergence of a really vital positive behavior on the part of your associates. It means avoiding threats that only instill fear and guilt and, instead, using criticism and reprimands in an affirmative manner."

"That sounds like a paradox, Ted. Can you explain?"

Punish Only When Positive Reinforcement Does Not Work and Behavior Is Truly Aversive

"We have some concrete suggestions we put into practice—and quite successfully. The first is to punish only when reinforcement doesn't work—only as a last resort—as in the case of *frequent* misbehavior. I ignore misbehavior that happens only once or very seldom. The only exception is the violation of a safety code, a code of business ethics or in cases where an associate abuses a customer or one of his or her colleagues. Another suggestion we follow is that punishment should be used *only when justified*—that is, when the behavior is truly aversive, not just aversive to *me.*"

"For example, Bob says, 'I think the president's really going to like this report,' and the manager says, 'Don't count on it. The old coot never likes anything.' Bob persists with 'Still, don't you think it's a pretty fair job?' The manager responds, 'Sure, but next time you could include an appendix and some backup statistics.' The manager punished Bob's performance because he is obviously bothered by his associate's confidence and success."

"So being a good manager means using responses that reinforce or are aversive to your associates, not to you?"

"Yes. Good management really is a variation on the golden rule: Treat others the way *they* want to be treated, not the way *you* want to be treated. Another suggestion is that *punishment should be personal.* It should be directed at a specific person, not a group. What we *don't do* is what a friend of mine told me happened in his company. A few people neglected to clean up the snack area, so management punished them all by closing the snack area for good. Why punish the many for the sins of the few? That's usually done because it's the easiest, not the best, solution."

Punishment Should Be Administered:

1. individually
2. privately
3. immediately
4. until positive results occur

"Do you have any other suggestions, Ted?"

"Yes. *We always punish in private, praise in public.* Nobody likes to be chewed out in front of others. It's humiliating and demeaning. Also, we guard against making the private public—for example, inviting an associate into your office and slamming the door in full view of his or her colleagues. Arrange a quiet conference after working hours."

"What else, Ted?"

"*Immediate punishment* is the most effective. The longer you ignore misbehavior, the harder it is to change. It's easiest to describe and deal with the behavior while it's fresh in everyone's mind."

"What if someone is so upset that he or she can't really hear the criticism? I have an associate like that, she gets very emotional."

"That's the one exception where it *is* best to let the distraught associate cool down before confronting him or her. We also use a tactic that behaviorists call *avoidance learning*."

"What does that mean?"

"Once you start an aversive stimulus, don't stop it until you get positive behavior. Or in plain English, we don't let people 'get away with it.'"

"Have you got an example?"

"Yes, I do. Remember Dave and the manager we talked about a few minutes ago?"

"I sure do. The manager backed off when Dave gave him the excuse routine."

"Right. But this time when Dave grouses about the research department's alleged tardiness, the manager says, 'And why did that present a problem?' Dave snaps back, 'I couldn't start the report on time.' The manager zeroes in with 'Why not? The data is designed only for the appendix.' Dave then backs down, saying 'I suppose you're right.' The manager finishes it off with 'Next time, you might consider talking to research and seeing if they can help us out.' This way he stops the punishment and reinforces Dave for accepting responsibility. In other words, the manager didn't let up until he heard a useful response. Managing, we must remember, is not searching for ways to be Mr. Nice Guy. It's getting your people to cooperate and produce good results."

"How do you do this in your company, Ted?"

"When there are performance problems with an associate, we first ask him to fill out a problem analysis worksheet. It includes the following:

1. A description of the problem
2. Identification of possible causes

3. Identification of possible solutions
4. Evaluation of these solutions
5. Actions to take to implement these solutions

"Then you discuss it with your associate?"

"Yes, but I do this informally, quietly, and without judging or faultfinding. I focus on the deed, not the doer. The problem analysis technique usually works."

"And if it doesn't?"

"Then, after an agreed-upon length of time, if there is no acceptable improvement or resolution of the problem, a probationary memorandum is prepared stating the problem and outlining steps to be taken to correct it within a time limit, usually 30 days."

"What if the terms are not met in 30 days?"

"Then, as stated in the memorandum, employment is terminated."

"Would it be possible for me to get copies of the problem analysis worksheet and a probationary memorandum?"

"Sure. I'll bring you copies next week."

"Thanks so much, Ted. What you've shared with me today confirms my belief that you have something I call leadership style."

"Thanks, Bill. I know there are democratic styles and authoritarian styles. I guess mine is more a situational style. I vary it with the person. If a person lacks motivation and needs praise, I provide it. I believe style in management comes from paying close attention to your associates' needs and deciding what you can provide to help them do their best job. After all, that's what leadership is all about: helping people to help themselves."

"Next week?"

"We'll build a positive culture! See you then."

(Sample)

Problem Analysis Worksheet

Name: Michael Smith Department: Customer Service
Position: Customer Service Rep Reports to: Jean Madden

1. Describe output gap specifically:

Desired output:

Answer 80 customer inquiry letters per week.

Actual output:

Answered 58 letters per week (average 1/1/92-7/1/92).

Gap or discrepancy:

22 letters per week.

2. Identify possible causes:

1. Need more technical information on company products.
2. Need better writing skills.
3. Need to organize time more effectively and eliminate interruptions from co-workers.

3. Identify alternative solutions:

1. Discuss products with managers of all departments.
2. Enroll in business writing course with community college.
3. Meet with co-workers to arrange for modification of interruptions and noise level.

4. Evaluate alternative solutions:

Alternative 1	Alternative 2	Alternative 3
Easy to implement but	Investigate	Discuss this with
will take time.	writing courses	my department
Expect full	in local schools	manager and
cooperation from	and colleges. Find	arrange to put on
department managers.	out cost of	agenda for next
Begin immediately to	courses and get	departmental
set up one-hour	suggestions/	meeting.
appointments with	evaluations from	
nine managers. Prepare	former students.	
preliminary draft of	Discuss with my	
my product knowledge	department	
of each department and	manager whether	
give to manager in	company may	
advance of interview.	defray all or	
Take careful notes and	part of cost of	
type up final draft to	writing course.	
submit to each manager		
for review, comments		
and corrections.		

5. Decide on course(s) of action:

Actions	Start Date	Completion Date
MAJOR: Increase customer	8/1/92	12/31/92
replies by 22 letters per		
week to a total of 80 letters		
per week.		
TO IMPLEMENT:		
1. Talk with department	8/1/92	9/1/92
managers concerning products.		
2. Enroll in writing course.	As soon as possible.	
3. Arrange with department	8/1/92	9/1/92
managers and co-workers to		
minimize interruptions and		
noise levels.		

Signed (Employee) /Date   Signed (Supervisor) /Date

Note: *The following page contains a blank form that may be reproduced for your personal use if you wish. Or, you may want to modify it and create your own.*

Problem Analysis Worksheet

Name: ______________________ Department: __________________
Position: ____________________ Reports to: ____________________

1. Describe output gap specifically:

Desired output:

____

Actual output:

____

Gap or discrepancy:

____

2. Identify possible causes:

____
____
____
____
____
____

3. Identify alternative solutions:

____
____
____
____
____
____

4. Evaluate alternative solutions:

Alternative 1	Alternative 2	Alternative 3

5. Decide on course(s) of action:

Actions	Start Date	Completion Date

Signed (Employee) /Date Signed (Supervisor) /Date

(Sample)

Probationary Memorandum

To: Doris Bates, Customer Service Rep
From: Helen Brown, Manager
Date: September 1, 1992
Re: 30-Day Probationary Period

NOTICE: As we have discussed, this notice is to serve as documentation of problems to be corrected during this 30-day probationary period (9/1/92-9/30/92). Following your present pattern, I do not find you to be productive nor effective in your position. You have been habitually late, which causes problems in performing your duties as a customer service representative, especially when calls begin coming into the offices for service at 8:30 a.m. There have been serious instances of miscommunication and lack of communication with me.

ACTIONS TO BE TAKEN:

1. You must be at your desk and ready to work at 8:30 every day.
2. Any sick-day absences must be accompanied by a written doctor's excuse when you return to work.
3. Personal telephone calls are not to exceed two per day and to last no more than two minutes each per company policy.
4. All duties and functions are to be completed on time per your job description.
5. Your appearance is to be appropriate to the work environment.
6. Any and all personal problems are to be handled outside the office.

COMPLIANCE: Your failure to comply with any of the above action items within the next 30 days will result in termination of employment. Prior to your release from this probationary period, we will meet with Betty Simms, Vice President, to review and discuss the above since no further probationary period regarding these matters will be extended.

____
Manager's Signature /Date

AGREEMENT:
I have read and do accept the terms as outlined above regarding my probationary period. I also understand if the terms are not met, I will be immediately subject to termination of employment.

____
Associate's Signature /Date

cc: Betty Simms, Vice President
Associate's File

Note: *The following page contains a blank form that may be reproduced for your personal use if you wish. Or, you may want to modify it and create your own.*

Probationary Memorandum

To:
From:
Date:
Re: 30-Day Probationary Period

NOTICE:

ACTIONS TO BE TAKEN:

COMPLIANCE: Your failure to comply with any of the above action items within the next 30 days will result in termination of employment. Prior to your release from this probationary period, we will meet with ________________, Vice President, to review and discuss the above since no further probationary period regarding these matters will be extended.

____
Manager's Signature /Date

AGREEMENT:
I have read and do accept the terms as outlined above regarding my probationary period. I also understand if the terms are not met, I will be immediately subject to termination of employment.

____
Associate's Signature /Date

cc: Vice President
Associate's File

15

Building a Positive Culture

"What's this 'positive culture' we're discussing today, Ted?"

"It's really the culmination of all we've been talking about, Bill. When we first started our discussions, you mentioned that you sensed a high level of vitality when you came to our offices. We believe that's true, and we're proud of it. A successful company has what I like to call a *culture of productivity* and high performance. This culture makes a strong statement about the company's purpose and its core values."

"And I suppose this positive culture is a trust builder?"

"Indeed it is. A strong culture creates a sense of reliability and confidence. Everyone knows exactly what the company stands for and what results are expected of them. Culture is part and parcel of the trust that glues an organization together."

"What would be your exact definition of the word culture, Ted?"

"It is everything that influences people's thoughts and behavior."

"Such as?"

"Examples of culture are corporate rites and rituals, an organization's physical setting, communication styles, company slogans, stories and symbols, company heroes and myths, and the way people dress and talk to outsiders, even their favorite sports and recreational activities."

"Could you give more specific examples?"

"Yes. A bank is a good example. There's a hush-hush atmosphere in the main office of a big bank. You see men and women wearing conservative gray or navy blue suits. There are quiet conversations behind closed doors and lunches at the finest restaurants. Customers are greeted graciously, and all the niceties of etiquette are meticulously observed."

"In other words, the bank projects an air of stability, security and tradition to its clientele."

"Right. The bank's culture communicates the message 'Don't worry; your money is safe with us. We know what we're doing. We've been doing it for years.' But let's look at a computer software company."

"You mean all hustle and bustle? Very informal?"

"Decidedly. Young men and women are huddled in front of computer screens engaged in heated discussion. They all look like math whizzes. Their dress is ultracasual—jeans, T-shirts, sneakers. The atmosphere is laid-back, collegial. It's hard to tell managers from workers. Everyone eats together in the company cafeteria or orders out for pizza."

"So there's a feeling of creativity and innovation there?"

"Yes. This culture says, 'Our products are the newest and the best. We're one step ahead of the competition and aim to stay that way.' The purpose of any culture, Bill, is to commit everyone to a common purpose, to encourage them to produce high-quality output and to train and educate them *all* to do this. In other words, culture is values and principles expressed symbolically."

A Successful Company's Culture Expresses Its Purpose and Core Values

"How do you mean, Ted?"

"A symbol is something that stands for something else, that sends a message about something else. The bankers' wardrobes are symbolic of maturity and wealth. The computer programmers' clothing is symbolic of casual creativity."

"Do you have symbols in your business?"

"Yes. Our Eagle awards are symbolic of values such as individuality and excellence. Neither good employees nor eagles flock. They are found one at a time, so we've chosen the eagle as the symbol for our employee awards program."

"I'm not sure we have a culture in our plant. Maybe we'd better start thinking about it."

"It's not a bad idea, Bill. Remember, being sensitive to culture means thinking on two levels—the surface and the symbolic. For instance, take a parking lot. If you're thinking only on the surface, a parking lot without assigned spaces is just a parking lot. If you're thinking symbolically, it's a statement of equality. As a plant manager, you can start by identifying values and norms in your company and begin building a culture that symbolizes them."

"Let's start with an explanation of what you mean by *values* and *norms.*"

"*Values* are principles or qualities people believe in because they think they're important—for example, quality, caring about customers, reliability and innovation. Norms are collective beliefs that all members of a group share."

"Then a good manager focuses on the key values and norms that support his or her company's goals?"

"Yes. Take honesty as an example. You put a high value on honesty and expect your associates to be honest in everything they do. But what happens if your associates share norms such as 'Pad expense accounts if you can get away with it,' 'Tell customers what they want to hear' or 'Don't tell the truth if it means rocking the boat'? If you want to build a culture in your plant that values honesty, you must identify conflicting norms and change them."

"That's easier said than done."

"Changing anything isn't easy, but changing a culture is especially hard. It takes time. I'm reminded of the CEO who turned to his assistant after listening to a speech on culture at a conference and said, 'I like this culture stuff. I want one installed by Monday.' It just doesn't happen that way."

"Is that because most people are reluctant to abandon thinking and behavior that stand in the way of change?"

"So true. They like the sense of belonging and approval they get by conforming to existing values and norms. Marching to a different drummer sounds better in a book than in an office or factory. Change involves risking the unknown, loss of status and a place in a group. It's a little frightening to have the familiar rug yanked out from under our feet."

"Does taking a risk also mean there's a chance we'll fail?"

"Yes. We don't want to be losers, so we fight to continue in the old rut. A company usually pays a high price for its reluctance to change. American auto companies, for example, eventually had to change in response to foreign competition and rebuild their cultures based on higher quality. And after the breakup, AT&T had to change from a near monopoly to a new culture of innovation and marketing."

"Are strong corporate cultures really a *sine qua non* for success?"

"Yes. They focus everyone's sights on core values. They are positive cultures of innovation, productivity and quality. Weak, negative cultures, however, result in stagnation, low productivity and low quality."

How To Build a Positive Culture

"I know that change is in order at my plant, so I'd like to find out how to begin changing and building a positive culture."

"Okay, Bill. First, assume that you're not fighting a war. Resistance to change is more passive than active. People just want to keep on doing what they're doing, good or bad, simply because it takes less energy and effort. Thus, without any weapons in hand, you can start to identify your existing culture and reward your associates for doing and saying things differently. Let them participate. People support what they help create and will feel less threatened by a process they have helped put in place themselves."

"Are there some specific steps I can take?"

"Yes. *First, find out where you are right now.* Keep your eyes and ears open. You won't hear your associates talking explicitly about workplace values and norms, but you will hear them talking about 'the way things are around here.' You may hear such statements as 'Don't worry about what to do; we'll tell you,' 'Buck management and you're asking for trouble,' 'Don't criticize the boss even if you think she's wrong,' 'Always go through channels even if it takes too long,' 'If you want productivity, fine, but don't expect quality to stay up to par' and 'If it ain't broke, don't fix it.'"

Steps to Building a Positive Culture

1. Find out what norms and values are shared by associates.
2. Compare norms with company's goals.
3. Symbolize norms and values you want to develop.

"Are these all *negative* norms?"

"Yes, but it's equally important to identify *positive* norms, so you can reward them. While you're listening, make sure your associates are communicating, too. Schedule a meeting to talk about culture. This gets your people thinking and talking about norms and values, and they don't feel they're being evaluated or judged. Remember, culture is a tool, not a club."

"What's the second step I can take to bring about this change in my plant?"

"Once you have uncovered norms and values shared by your associates, compare them to your goals and the demands of your environment. Which ones contribute to productivity? Which ones undermine it? Which ones no longer fit tomorrow's challenges? Which ones are crucial to success? But always remember that *participation* is an important factor, and you can't change things overnight. Wholesale reorganizations rarely work."

"And the third step, Ted?"

"The third step is to symbolize the norms and values you want to develop. Reward what you want and actively discourage what you

don't want. You will then find yourself behaving in new ways to symbolize the values and norms you want."

"Isn't symbolizing a little difficult? It's not something I've been doing?"

"Once you get into the *habit* of seeing everything symbolically, you won't have trouble with symbolic thinking. Everything you are doing now—meetings, memos, talks—will begin to convey values. And you'll change the way you talk about norms."

"For example?"

"Take the negative statements and turn them into positive ones. Instead of saying 'Don't worry about what to do; we'll tell you,' you can say 'Everyone here makes decisions important to them.' Or instead of saying 'Always go through channels', you can say 'Bypass normal channels when the situation warrants.'"

"Are there other examples?"

"Yes. Get rid of assigned parking spaces and private offices. Set up plenty of conference rooms to encourage your associates to get together and communicate openly and honestly. Increase the amount of time you spend talking with your associates about their problems. Work on positive slogans, signs and awards."

"I know you do all this."

"One reason we accomplish so much is that there's strong agreement about our most important value—helping small business owners and executives. We are dedicated to fostering the entrepreneurial spirit by providing ideas, information, forms, methods, techniques and financial advice to small businesses to help them unlock their human and financial capital and *succeed.* A good example of our shared values is a statement our distribution center manager wrote for the dedication of our new warehouse, and all our employees took pleasure in signing it. I just happen to have it with me."

"I'd like to hear it, Ted."

"It reads as follows: 'We, the employees of Enterprise Ventures, Inc., express our confidence and support in the continued growth of the company and ourselves as we dedicate our new warehouse to the spirit of free enterprise. As we celebrate our prosperity, may this new facility symbolize our dedication to working together in championing our customers' dreams of success.'"

"I like that. May I have a copy?"

"I'll have one made for you, Bill, and will bring it next Wednesday, at which time I think we can wrap up all we've talked about over the past weeks."

"I'll look forward to that—though not to the end of our lunches together. You know, Ted, maybe you ought to put this all together in a book!"

I smiled, "Maybe I will! See you next week, Bill."

16

Putting It into Practice

Since this was our last lunch together for a while, we decided to splurge on the Dover sole.

"Ted, I'm really anxious to put into practice in my printing plant the concepts we have discussed over the past few weeks. Some I've already tested—rather successfully, I might say."

"There is no reason why you can't put them *all* to work for you. I think you will be amazed at the improvements you will begin to see, many of them right away. Remember, though, there aren't any instant solutions or surefire gimmicks."

"I know. But I can see that there are a few secrets that appear to guarantee success."

Trust Building Comes from Doing Little Things Better

"Answering and acting on questions such as the following builds trust: Does your company have a meaningful mission? Does each member of your company have a meaningful personal mission? Do your associates have a way to keep score? Are they rewarded for successful performance? Are you really listening to them? Do your managers provide their associates with the input they need to do a good job? Are you building a strong business team in which *everyone* participates, communicates and innovates? Do your associates feel trusted and respected as adults? Have they been encouraged to develop the confidence it takes to conquer challenges? Does your corporate culture reinforce norms and values critical to success? Do your managers lead with trust and integrity? If you can answer 'yes' to all these questions, you are on the road to greater trust and productivity."

The Power of a Positive Culture

"I can see, Ted, that the power of a positive culture is of paramount importance."

"Yes, and it can turn a company into a strong, vital, productive organization."

"Will a positive culture increase sales and profits? We'd like to see that happen."

"Yes, it will. In my company we achieve a remarkable level of annual sales and profits with a limited number of employees. And our profits are high."

"But you have *quality* products and services."

"We do, and that's important, Bill. I'm not suggesting that the concepts we have talked about automatically spell success. You obviously need top-notch products and/or services competitively priced. I believe your plant offers these."

"I think we do. In fact, I *know* we do, and we have good people producing them."

Attitude + Productivity = Success

"Your success depends on the attitudes and productivity of your associates. Just picture what you can achieve if the attitude and spirit of your key people—as well as your own—rises to new, higher levels. By practicing the principles we have discussed and reshaping your culture, you will enjoy better communication and richer human relationships with your staff. These principles work whether an organization employs six people or six thousand."

"I know they'll work for me, Ted. And I know we need to accomplish this by evolution, not revolution. As the saying goes, 'The mills of the gods grind slowly.'"

"But not *too* slowly, Bill. A good way to get the ball rolling is to call your people together and tell them you have some good news to share. Explain that you want to make the plant a better place to work and ask them if they'd like to be involved. Tell them you need *everyone's* help."

"I know I need my associates' wholehearted support and total commitment to build mutual trust."

"Right, and you will trust, identify and reward each associate's output."

"And reach decisions by consensus?"

"Yes. You'll find, of course, that your associates' reactions may vary, although the majority will probably begin to participate positively and enthusiastically right away. Share the ideas we have talked about. I'm going to give you some exercises I have brought with me today to help you analyze just where your company now stands. We call these exercises our Trust Assessment Survey (see Appendix A). Associates should answer each question on the survey in terms of (1) their own departments and (2) the company as a whole. You may, of course, amend and/or modify the survey to fit your own business."

"I will, Ted, and if you agree, I'll keep a progress log to share with you from time to time—say, once a month. Okay?"

"Good idea, Bill. And I'll be eager to follow it."

"Does that mean we can continue our lunches on a monthly basis for updating and input from you, as well as the pleasure of your company?"

"There's nothing I'd like better."

"Thanks again, Ted. See you a month from today."

"Great. And lots of luck on your new venture, Bill!"

Appendix A
Trust Assessment Survey

The following is the Trust Assessment Survey discussed in Chapter 16.

It is useful to administer the survey when:

1. Initiating your management program. It will provide a starting place for improvement and let you know where concentrated effort may be needed.
2. You feel significant changes have been made and you want employee feedback to help measure if progress is made.
3. Annually, as a matter of routine. Changes in mix of management and staff may produce results that are surprising.
4. Three months after any major changes in top management or policy. You will get more feedback after associates have had the opportunity to adapt to the change.

In evaluating results, score each survey by adding the number of 4s, 3s, 2s and 1s for each survey together and divide by the number of surveys to get an average score for the department and/or company.

Focus closer attention on those questions where a high percentage of associates gave a low score to a particular question or questions. This may be key to determining problem areas that require changes in management behavior.

Following the survey is a score sheet to assist managers in tabulating results.

Trust Assessment Survey

The purpose of this survey is to help us measure the degree of trust in our organization. It is important for you to be as honest as you can when filling out the questionnaire. Respond as you actually see the situation, not as you wish it were.

The results of this survey will be held completely confidential. You need not sign your name, just your department. In this way, we'll be able to compare perceptions among departments.

DIRECTIONS:

Circle the number from 1 to 4 that best represents your response.

1	means	*never*
2	means	*occasionally*
3	means	*frequently*
4	means	*always*

Please answer in Column A how you see the situation in the company as a whole; in Column B, how you see the situation in your own department.

If you feel you cannot respond to a statement, please leave it blank. Do not guess.

		Company	**Department**
1.	Is there a high level of mutual trust?	1 2 3 4	1 2 3 4
2.	Do we work together as a team—i.e., is there a high degree of mutual support?	1 2 3 4	1 2 3 4
3.	Do managers expect associates to succeed and communicate a degree of confidence in their ability to do so?	1 2 3 4	1 2 3 4
4.	Is there a general sense of confidence and optimism?	1 2 3 4	1 2 3 4

		Company	Department
5.	Is there a strong sense of purpose that managers communicate to their associates?	1 2 3 4	1 2 3 4
6.	Are managers committed to productivity, making sure that everyone understands the concept of productivity?	1 2 3 4	1 2 3 4
7.	Are the company's main goals and direction clearly stated and communicated to everyone?	1 2 3 4	1 2 3 4
8.	Is the company committed to a few key values that are clearly understood by everyone?	1 2 3 4	1 2 3 4
9.	Does everyone feel free to raise and discuss the company's mission and its important values?	1 2 3 4	1 2 3 4
10.	When clarifying and developing values, do managers involve everyone?	1 2 3 4	1 2 3 4
11.	Can everyone identify with and understand the company's values?	1 2 3 4	1 2 3 4
12.	Is there an effective system for setting personal goals?	1 2 3 4	1 2 3 4
13.	Are goals developed primarily by the person(s) who must achieve them?	1 2 3 4	1 2 3 4
14.	Has a useful measurement system been developed?	1 2 3 4	1 2 3 4
15.	Is the measurement system seen as a useful tool, not a club?	1 2 3 4	1 2 3 4
16.	Does the measurement system allow associates to measure quality, not just quantity of output?	1 2 3 4	1 2 3 4

		Company	Department
17.	Are measurements developed mainly by the people who must use them?	1 2 3 4	1 2 3 4
18.	When associates perform successfully, do they earn rewards that are personally important?	1 2 3 4	1 2 3 4
19.	Is the work environment designed to provide the kinds of incentives and rewards that group members want?	1 2 3 4	1 2 3 4
20.	Do managers encourage associates to discuss the rewards they favor?	1 2 3 4	1 2 3 4
21.	Do managers share power with associates by providing maximum responsibility, decision-making authority, and resources?	1 2 3 4	1 2 3 4
22.	Are managers and associates honest—i.e., do they say what they mean and do what they say?	1 2 3 4	1 2 3 4
23.	Do supervisors and colleagues encourage the expression of feelings and ideas?	1 2 3 4	1 2 3 4
24.	When communicating, do managers and employees reflect verbally their understanding of what has been said?	1 2 3 4	1 2 3 4
25.	When talking to managers or other colleagues, do associates feel free to express emotions without fear of negative feedback?	1 2 3 4	1 2 3 4
26.	Do managers and associates try to understand what's being said before criticizing or judging?	1 2 3 4	1 2 3 4
27.	Are problems resolved promptly rather than swept under the rug?	1 2 3 4	1 2 3 4

		Company	Department
28.	When disagreements occur, do managers encourage all interested parties to participate in resolving them?	1 2 3 4	1 2 3 4
29.	When dealing with conflicts, do group leaders focus on the problem, not the person?	1 2 3 4	1 2 3 4
30.	Are conflicts resolved by working toward either compromise or consensus?	1 2 3 4	1 2 3 4
31.	When seeking solutions to problems, do group leaders encourage members to generate many alternatives, rather than to impose either/or solutions?	1 2 3 4	1 2 3 4
32.	Are associates given the opportunity to participate in decisions important to them?	1 2 3 4	1 2 3 4
33.	Do managers perceive everyone to be potentially creative and innovative?	1 2 3 4	1 2 3 4
34.	Do managers solicit ideas about improving work-related problems?	1 2 3 4	1 2 3 4
35.	Do managers listen carefully to ideas and suggestions from everyone, not just a few?	1 2 3 4	1 2 3 4
36.	Is information necessary to effective job performance consistently provided?	1 2 3 4	1 2 3 4
37.	Do managers accept and even encourage associates to make mistakes?	1 2 3 4	1 2 3 4
38.	Do managers encourage calculated risk taking?	1 2 3 4	1 2 3 4

		Company	Department
39.	Is good performance positively reinforced—i.e., do managers try to "catch people doing something right"?	1 2 3 4	1 2 3 4
40.	When reinforcement is given, is it unconditional (no if, but or however statements added)?	1 2 3 4	1 2 3 4
41.	Is constructive feedback frequently and consistently provided?	1 2 3 4	1 2 3 4
42.	Is feedback given not only when performance is poor or excellent but whenever feedback is requested or could be useful?	1 2 3 4	1 2 3 4
43.	Is feedback in the form of either positive reinforcement or punishment always specific—i.e., does it refer to specific behavior?	1 2 3 4	1 2 3 4
44.	Do managers try to make performance evaluations relaxed and anxiety free?	1 2 3 4	1 2 3 4
45.	Are formal performance evaluations scheduled regularly?	1 2 3 4	1 2 3 4
46.	Are informal evaluations offered whenever requested?	1 2 3 4	1 2 3 4
47.	When punishment is used, do managers explain the specific behavior being punished?	1 2 3 4	1 2 3 4
48.	When managers use punishment, do they offer the associate ample opportunity to discuss the problem behavior and why action is being taken?	1 2 3 4	1 2 3 4

		Company	Department
49.	When using punishment or communicating negative feedback, do managers reaffirm confidence in the associate?	1 2 3 4	1 2 3 4
50.	Do associates feel free to discuss, criticize and evaluate the company's culture and to discuss its basic direction and purpose?	1 2 3 4	1 2 3 4

Score Sheet for Trust Assessment Survey

Survey Question	Participant								Survey Question	Participant							
1.									26.								
2.									27.								
3.									28.								
4.									29.								
5.									30.								
6.									31.								
7.									32.								
8.									33.								
9.									34.								
10.									35.								
11.									36.								
12.									37.								
13.									38.								
14.									39.								
15.									40.								
16.									41.								
17.									42.								
18.									43.								
19.									44.								
20.									45.								
21.									46.								
22.									47.								
23.									48.								
24.									49.								
25.									50.								
									Totals:								

Department Average = __________

Appendix B
Letter from Ted Nicholas

Dear Reader,

As you begin to build a higher degree of trust in your company, you will have happier, more productive people and a more profitable company. Another benefit is that internal communications will vastly improve. This delights most entrepreneurs.

However, if the task of adjusting your management style, even slightly, seems formidable, don't be too surprised. It's not unusual to feel a bit nervous whenever a new management approach is attempted. I certainly feel that way whenever I try something new.

But let's keep things in perspective. One of the beauties of creating a trust-building environment is that there is simply no downside risk. You have everything to gain and nothing to lose, even if you make a few mistakes along the way.

A simple way many readers have found to gain the support of their employees is to ask them to read a copy of this book. Suggest this before shifting any procedures and before they complete the Trust Assessment Survey. Most of your employees' questions will be answered, and they probably will feel more at ease.

Nothing is as assuredly rewarding in the business world as building a great team of people as you move toward realizing your management goals.

I extend my best wishes to you in your quest of becoming a better manager. To know that I have played some part, however minor, in helping you build your business through more effective humanistic management is highly satisfying to me.

For more detailed information on available services and consultation, write or fax: Nicholas Direct, Inc., 19918 Gulf Boulevard, No. 7, Indian Shores, FL 34635, fax 1-813-596-6900. I'll be glad to place your name on our mailing list to receive information concerning books, articles and newsletters we publish, as well as seminars we conduct. I'm also interested in the experiences of my readers, so I invite you to write me concerning yours at the above address.

Sincerely,

Ted Nicholas

Index